KABOING!

50 IDEAS THAT WILL

SPRINGBOARD YOU INTO

ACADEMIC GREATNESS

By John A. Chuback, M.D., FACS

Kaboing! 50 Ideas That Will Springboard You to Academic Greatness
by John A. Chuback, M.D., FACS

ISBN: 978-1-312-93196-1

This edition published May 2015.

Printed in the United States of America.

TABLE OF CONTENTS

"I am a part of all that I have met."
— ALFRED TENNYSON

INTRODUCTION

I have spent the last 42 of my 45 years in some sort of formal academic training. Clearly, certain periods of my scholastic life were more intensive than others. For example, it wouldn't be fair to compare my first year of nursery school at age 3 to my final year of cardiovascular surgical training at age 33. Nevertheless, both of those years had their own set of challenges, obstacles and lessons.

We should always be learning. In my opinion, a life that lacks a steady advancement in knowledge, experience and competence is incomplete. There is a certain satisfaction that one only achieves through growing and maturing intellectually. Education is a wonderful journey, full of joy and enlightenment.

What I share with you in this book is simply a collection of stories, parables and events from my own life experience. Everything I include here has helped to shape who I am as a student and as a human being. My sincere hope is that these pages will have an impact on you and make you think more deeply about your education. I believe it is always useful to see things in a new light or from a new perspective. My feeling is that if even one of these 50 chapters can help you see things differently, so that it helps you become more successful in school, then I've accomplished something powerful. My journey has been long, and at times arduous, but I wouldn't trade it for the world. The process of personal development that a formal education brings out in the individual is truly invaluable. I wish you great success in your own pursuit of knowledge and hope that it adds as much richness to your life as it has mine. If you apply the ideas outlined in the following pages, your academic performance is sure to go *KABOING!*

CHAPTER 1

SIT

L et me share with you a vivid memory. It was July 1st, 1995, the first day of my General Surgical Residency at Monmouth Medical Center in Long Branch, N.J. All of the residents were gathered in the surgical library. The surgical library was a beautiful room with a large conference table, bookshelves on two sides and a bank of windows on the third wall. There were a couple of computer stations, and along the front wall was a white board for teaching and a retractable projection screen. Around the table and along the perimeter of the room we all sat. The rookies like me appeared a bit anxious and formal with our newly acquired white coats and snugly cinched neck ties. The more senior residents, some of whom had been working to earn their diploma for as long as 10 years, displayed varying degrees of calm, arrogance, hostility, fatigue, burnout and boredom in anticipation of what was to come.

From within the surgical library, one could see two doors. Both were presently closed. It was July and certainly a bit stuffy. This was one of the few days ever that all of the residents were assembled in one place. They had come back from all of our affiliated hospitals to be present for the annual greeting that was about to be given by the Chairman of the Department of Surgery. Many of these young men and women had not slept or bathed in two or three days. Undergarments had not been changed, teeth had not been brushed, and deodorant had not been reapplied. The rest of us were freshly adorned with perfumes and colognes. The odor that lingered in the air conjured up an image of a room shared by a cowboy and a dance hall girl in a brothel in the Wild West.

One door was the door back out the hallway, which through a labyrinth of unfamiliar turns and stairways, ultimately led to the hospital. The other door was the door to the Chairman's office. Without any particular fanfare or warning, the door opened and Dr. Charles Sills emerged from his private office. He closed the door behind him and took a seat at the head of the table, a seat which had been conspicuously left vacant despite the fact that the room was packed to standing room only magnitude.

Sills was a small man who carried with him an enormous presence. The room became silent and still as he entered. He was always impeccably dressed in a suit and tie. Charles Sills was not a particularly good-looking man, at first glance that is. He had a somewhat severe looking face with exaggerated features. His nose was fairly large, his mouth prominent and his lips thick. His hair was thinning, but impeccably groomed, always freshly cut and very soft looking. His face was wrinkled with age, but came across as experienced and wise rather than old. His skin was supple. He was always clean-shaven. His teeth were a bit crooked and slightly yellowed. Despite this, there was no denying that he was clearly a very charismatic and attractive man. I had no way of knowing it at the time, but over the subsequent years, he would become one of three or four men, in addition to my father, who would have a major impact on shaping my life.

Without any particularly warm welcome, he began to speak. His Bronx accent was still apparent but somewhat softened after 25 years of residing in a central Jersey shore town. He made his message clear. He was a man who never parsed words. He said, "This is graduate level education. Some of you may be under the impression that this is a teaching hospital. If so, you have been misinformed and are mistaken. This is, however, a learning hospital. You are here to learn. There is much to be learned here. But, if you expect me to come in here and sit down and read the textbook of surgery to you, you will be sorely disappointed". He then pointed to the door through which he had entered and continued, "That is the door to my office. You'll notice that it is closed. I do not have an open door policy. If you have a problem of any kind, I do not want to know about it. If you are a first year resident and you have a problem you can't handle on your own, ask a second year resident for guidance. If you are a second year resident and you can't solve the problem, go to a third year resident for more help. I think you see my point. The only resident I ever want knocking on that door is the Chief Resident. He or she may knock because they can't solve the problems of the surgical service. And, if the Chief Resident does come to see me, I will see it as a failure on their part. They should keep in mind that in 12 short months they will be out practicing surgery and there will be no door to knock upon. You are here to learn the art of surgery and the discipline of independence."

He went on to talk about his expectations in terms of our

schedule and anticipated work ethic. He said, "All things going perfectly, you will be in this hospital, or one of our affiliated hospitals, every day for the next five years. You will be here either because you are working, or because you are so sick that you are in the hospital as a patient." By this time, I'm sure you can imagine he had my complete attention. I was focused on his every word. I had never heard a first day welcome speech anything like this. I had had many first day talks. There was the first day of school, the first day of football practice, the first day of cub scouts, the first day of medical school et cetera, but none of them was anything like this!

Finally, Dr. Sills wrapped up his talk with the brief explanation of how he became academically, professionally, and financially successful. It went like this, "Obviously, when you look at me you can surmise that I didn't become a Board Certified General Surgeon, a Board Certified Thoracic Surgeon, the Chairman of the Department of Surgery, and a successful businessman because of my good looks." Then he spoke the words I will never forget, the words that have forever changed my life. These were the words I wished I had heard 20 years earlier, and the words I am now going to share with you. He said, "I am who I am because I out-sat everybody."

Out-sat everybody? Did he say out-sat everybody? What the hell did he mean by that? How do you become a doubly Board Certified surgeon and a millionaire by out-sitting everybody? Fortunately, he went on to explain. "You see what I did my entire life was get to the library first, sit down, and begin to read. Then the other good students would arrive. Those who cared enough to go the library to study that is. And I would continue to sit and read. We would all be there together… sitting and reading. And then I would wait for them to leave, one by one. I would read until it was just me and one other person. And I would keep reading. Then the last person would pack up his belongings and leave. And I would be all alone again. It was at that point that I would look at the clock for the first time. I would take note of whatever time it was and read for 10 more minutes. Then, and only then, I would get up and leave. I owe all of my success to out-sitting the competition."

I particularly like to share this experience with young people. They usually think that the "smartest" kid in the class is the most successful student. My children have always come home with the following story, "Joe's a genius! He doesn't study at all yet he aces every calculus exam!" We've all heard these tales. Well, even if it were true that "Joe" was born somehow knowing European history, Latin, or quantum mechanics, the rest of us are not that lucky. The great majority of successful students will tell you that they read, and read, and read. I learned in my life to read like I was studying a script for a play. I would work my hardest to memorize every single word of every line of the book if time allowed. There are no short cuts. Rule number one in being a great student: you have to read like crazy!

CHAPTER 2

BIRD

Allow me to begin this chapter by telling you a bit about my father. He has been by far the most important role model in my life. His profound passion for education makes up the fabric of his being. As you will see, he will be mentioned frequently throughout the pages of this book. It will be my pleasure to share with you just a small fraction of what I have learned from him over the years.

My father was born in Iran in 1928. This was during The Shah's era when relations with America were excellent. His parents had both died by the time he was 12 years old and he was raised by his older brother, aunts and uncles. He attended medical school in Shiraz and then came to the United States in 1958 as class valedictorian for post-graduate medical education. He trained at Hahnemann Medical College in Philadelphia as an obstetrician/gynecologist and married my mother who was an American-born registered nurse of German and Swedish descent. At risk of sounding biased, I would attest that he is a brilliant and fascinating man with a work ethic second to none.

Growing up, my father and I would spend countless hours sitting at the kitchen table together. He would drink Persian-style tea, recite Persian poetry, sing Persian love songs, and teach philosophy. I would sit and listen. Unusual, you say? Perhaps, but that was my childhood. I would say 95% of the time I actually spent with my father growing up was at the kitchen table just as I have described. We spent a lot of time together. It was wonderful. Every child should be so blessed. My father was otherwise working. He had a medical office on the ground floor of our house, so between patients he would come upstairs and sit at the kitchen table and drink tea. In the Persian culture, tea is the hot beverage of choice. Coffee is rarely drunk, and tea is never served with milk. Classically the tea is served in a small glass, never a ceramic cup or mug. A cube of sugar is placed between the teeth and the hot elixir is sipped gradually, melting the sweet lump in the mouth. It's quite a cultural spectacle.

Much of the philosophical teaching was done in the form of parables. They would be repeated countless times over the years, ingraining their moral into the mind of the young listener. One of my favorites has come to be the story of the bird in the ice storm. It has particular relevance for young people. It can be applied to many situations in life, but for the purpose of this book, I will use it as a teaching tool with regard to academic excellence.

As Dad told it, the story goes something like this: Once upon a time there was a little song bird which was flying high above the jungle floor on a beautiful sunny day. As often happens in tropical climates, from out of nowhere a fierce storm blew in. Rain quickly turned to hail and ice. In moments, the little bird's wings became completely encased in ice. He was unable to fly and began hurling out of the sky as a solid ball of ice. Finally, he fell to the jungle floor, unable to breathe inside the block of ice. He was sure to die. But, alas, as he was beginning to suffocate, by chance an elephant strode directly over him and at the same moment relieved his bowels! A massive deposit of warm fecal material landed directly on the ice-encased creature. The warm feces almost instantly melted the ice, freeing the bird from his frigid tomb. Lying in a puddle of putrid mud, the bird began to chirp and sing loudly with glee, realizing that he was saved! Well, with that, a leopard who was walking in the nearby brush heard the little bird's song careening through the jungle. He moved in to investigate. There on the jungle floor he spotted the little bird with wet, stool-laden feathers. The bird was too soaked to fly away. The big cat carefully pawed the bird out of the noxious puddle and into a nice green patch of grass. He then proceeded to lick him clean. Once the bird was spotless, with his brightly colored feathers glistening in the sun, the predator tore him apart with his massive claws and ate him in a single bite.

The moral of the story is simple and threefold. First, in life not everyone who craps on you is your enemy. Second, not everyone who pulls you out of the crap and cleans you up is your friend. And third, when things are going your way, keep your mouth shut! What, you might ask, does any of this have to do with doing well in school and becoming a professional and having a wonderful career? I'll tell you. When we are young, we often think that when our parents tell us to go and study, they are doing us harm. We think, "Man, they never let me have any fun!" In a way, we see them as crapping on us, when in reality they may be saving our lives. There are many examples of this kind of interaction between parent and child. Just for the sake of providing a few, how about: "be home by eleven," "no, you can't sleep over," "go do your homework," "go read a book," "go work on your term paper," and so on and so forth. On the other hand, we often see the "friend" who calls and says, "let's go to the party," "we'll study another day," "we have plenty of time," "YOLO! you only live once!" as the good guy who's dragging us out of the crap and cleaning us up. When faced with these situations, never forget about the little bird in the ice storm! Never mistake your friend for your enemy or your enemy for your friend.

CHAPTER 3

FIVE

My sister Lily was a great inspiration to me academically during my early years. She was also the first one who laughed at my jokes and helped me believe that I was funny. Lil is 5 years older than me, but that has nothing to do with the title of this chapter: Five. What is important is that when she went off to college at New York University, she and I would talk frequently over the telephone. During these big sister-little brother chats, she would share with me advice on how I could do well in school. One of the adages she shared with me one evening was the following: "He who shall thrive must rise at five, while he who has thriven may rise at seven." As with many of the fables, and parables I share in this book, I often am unaware of the original source. To me, what is most important is my memory of how I came to learn them and my special relationships with the people who shared them with me. In the case of this quote, I did a bit of research and found that this proverb could be found in The Nursery Rhyme Book, edited by Andrew Lang in 1897. The original rhyme was as follows:

He that would thrive
Must rise at five;
He that hath thriven
May lie till seven;
And he that by the plow would thrive,
Himself must either hold or drive.

The last pair of lines is a wonderful addition to the version I had learned from Lil, although they were certainly implied in her rendition as well. The lesson here is obvious; if one wishes to be successful, one should get an early start on the day and get to work. Certainly, this advice was essential to my personal success and career choice. Throughout my seven years of surgical residency and fellowship we often rose before 5, and in fact spent many days and nights without sleeping at all. The reality is, like it or not, that successful people just plain outwork the rest of the crowd much of the time. Essential to the concept is that no one else can do your work for you, or plow your fields. To gain the bounty of the harvest, you yourself must sow the seed. Laziness is rarely, if ever, rewarded in the real world. So if you desire academic achievement and you yearn to be a winner, when setting your alarm clock, give me five!

CHAPTER 4

POWER

When my father was growing up as a child in Iran, every book that was published had a picture of the King and the slogan "Knowledge is power" printed on the title page. This was clearly meant to inspire the people of the country to pursue education as a means of attaining a higher station in life. I believe my father did find inspiration in that credo as a lad in the old country. Growing up, Dad used to tell us repeatedly that knowledge is power. This is a common phrase, which I am sure is prevalent in many cultures around the world. But is the phrase accurate? At face value it is quite logical and serves to be very motivational. But, when we dig a little deeper, does it really carry any weight? The answer is, probably not. The reality is that knowledge in and of itself does not give one any more power than the uninformed or ignorant. Truth be told, knowledge, only when put into action, is power. In other words, just knowing a bunch of stuff is not enough to make one powerful. We have all met people who have a wealth of knowledge, but are also chronically out of work and financially destitute. He or she may be a great teammate in a hotly contested game of Trivial Pursuit, but this is not a position in life I would wish on anyone.

For example, possessing a vast knowledge of engineering is wonderful, but in and of itself quite useless. On the other hand, if one puts that knowledge into action and designs a bridge which later connects two bodies of land so that food, fuel and other commodities can reach a population that had been previously without such resources... this is power. As another example, I believe that the knowledge one can acquire through reading this book is potentially very powerful, but if one elects not to put any of the tools and techniques described here into practice, one will see no change in their academic performance. What power does a highly educated surgeon have who spends years learning anatomy, physiology and technical maneuvers if he or she never operates on a patient? Essentially none.

The take home message from this chapter is obvious. Education and knowledge are terrific, but unless they are applied in some constructive manner, they do not amount to much. Knowledge, when put into action, is perhaps the most powerful force in the universe. This is why my father and many other immigrants that are fortunate enough to move to the United States believe in pursuing a formal profession, whether it be medicine, law, dentistry, accounting, engineering, etc. Newcomers to the country recognize that such skillsets allow one an opportunity to exercise their knowledge in some productive and useful way. Often, it is easier to obtain gainful employment when one has a professional degree. Of course, many individuals do well as entrepreneurs and build terrifically lucrative private enterprises from nothing but sheer determination and hard work; but, the path to such success is much more arcane. One who possesses a vast knowledge in a given subject, coupled with a traditional profession, can deliver earning power with much more predictability than one who lacks one or both of these assets.

CHAPTER 5

FORTUNE

When I was a resident in general surgery I had a professor who was a very talented vascular surgeon and a very important mentor to me. His name, Dr. George Constantinopoulos, was almost as difficult to spell as vascular surgery is to perform. Although I had no difficulty pronouncing his name, which was rich with history, with his permission I affectionately referred to him as "Dr. C". This was done simply in the interest of saving time. Let's face it, that name has 6 syllables and life is short. Because I was going to undertake a cardiovascular surgery fellowship following completion of my general surgical residency, I spent as much time as I could with this particularly gifted surgeon. He possessed many of the skills that I would need to master in order to be successful in my cardiovascular training and in my career. As a means of acquiring this specialized knowledge, I spent as much time with him as I possibly could. There was only one rub; this particular surgeon, although very capable technically and intellectually, was a stern taskmaster. Almost none of the residents wanted to work with him. He could be highly critical in the operating room if any moves were considered by him to deviate from a very strict standard.

In our fifth and final year of surgical residency, every chief resident spent 4 months on Dr. C's service. The Chief Resident would operate with him every day, doing all of his cases under his direct supervision. Well, it turned out that I spent 5 ½ months with this virtuoso because the Chief Resident who had been on his service called me the day that he satisfied all of his requirements for vascular operations and asked if I would switch with him. I was happy to let that resident take over control of the general surgical team and I headed over to vascular a month and a half early. While working together, Dr. C and I performed an enormous number of operations. With time, I became a bit of a golden boy in his eyes and we worked together seamlessly and joyfully until the time I graduated. We remain good friends and mutually respectful colleagues until this day.

As you might have guessed from his surname, Dr. Constantinopoulos was of Greek descent. In fact he was born and raised in Greece and came to the United States, much like my own father, after medical school for his residency training. He was quite proud of his rich Greek cultural background and history. My father being Persian led to many wonderful discussions of shared histories inside and outside of the O.R. One day during a challenging vascular reconstruction I happened to ask my teacher, "Dr. C, these are such amazing operations, why is it that so many of the residents want to avoid working with you? They have no idea what they are missing out on!" With that, Dr. C momentarily looked across at me over his magnifying loupes and said, "Yanni (Greek for John), when the student is ready, the teacher will appear." "Man!" I thought, "that's deep." Then I asked, "Is that a quote from Plato or Socrates, Dr. C?" "No", he responded,

"I actually read that in a fortune cookie in a Chinese restaurant." And he was serious! We both burst out in laughter. It's a funny moment I'll never forget, but it is an incredibly important lesson.

The real essence of the quote is that no matter how talented your teacher is, if you don't expose yourself to their lessons, you can't learn anything from them. If you are going to let fear of criticism keep you away from a genius in any field, then you can never grow from what they have to share with you. Often, the best teachers are the most rigorous. Don't let intimidation steer you away from the best educators. Embrace the wisdom of the sages you meet in life. If you will allow yourself to be a student, then and only then can the guru become your teacher.

CHAPTER 6

TROUBLE

So many of the great life lessons I learned came as a result of my rigorous surgical training. The concept shared in this chapter is yet another one of those. I had a professor named Donald Brief who was the Chairman of the Department of Surgery at Beth Israel Hospital in Newark, N.J. Dr. Brief was another brilliant man with whom I had the good fortune to work. He had an Ivy League education and was an exceptionally skillful surgeon. He had an extraordinary knowledge of human anatomy, and therefore demonstrated no fear in the operating room, no matter how complex the case at hand.

As I already mentioned we would spend 4 months of our final year of training on the vascular surgical service, and another four months on the general surgical clinic service. The remaining four months were spent working with Dr. Brief at Newark Beth Israel running his team. This meant that essentially every day you would be working alongside him and performing all of his cases under his direct supervision. As with Dr. C., this was very much an apprenticeship with a master craftsman prior to going out into the real world. As the Chief Resident, I had the authority to choose to do any operation with any surgeon that was on the O.R. schedule for that given day. For this reason, I would not be with Dr. Brief every day, but the lion's share of my time was spent one on one with the master himself for those 4 months.

Dr. Brief taught me that there are two major philosophies in life. This lesson has served me ever since, and I believe it will serve you as well if you truly take its meaning to heart. On the first day that I joined Dr. Brief on his service, he invited me downstairs in the hospital where there was a small coffee shop. We sat together at a little table and he bought me breakfast. We chatted a bit about his expectations for the coming four months. This was a wonderful rite of passage for each new Chief Resident serving with this great man. Just before getting up from the table to go to the floors and begin my morning rounds, Dr. Brief said, "John, in these next four months I'm going to teach you how to stay out of trouble in the operating room, and I'm going to leave up to the other surgeons to teach you how to get out of trouble in the operating room."

"Wow!" I thought to myself, "what an incredible way of look-ing at things. I have to be sure to never forget that statement." Well, it turned out I wouldn't have to worry about forgetting that concept. The next morning I arrived in the O.R. to join Dr. Brief for his morning case. As we washed our hands at the scrub sink just outside the operating room door, we chatted a bit about the patient, her diagnosis, and our operative plan for the day. Dr. Brief quizzed me a little on the pertinent anatomy and various steps in the proposed procedure to ensure that I was ready to per-form the operation. And then as he rinsed his hands under the water he looked over at me and said, "John, today I'm going to show you how to stay out of trouble, I'll leave to the other guys to show you how to get out of trouble." And despite the fact that he was wearing a surgical, cap, mask and his magnifying loupes, I could see a wry smile in the old fox's eyes as he turned away and walked into the operating room. Every time we scrubbed for a case during that four month stretch, he shared that message with me. And, I must say, he kept his promise. We had an amazing run together. The surgeries were clean and precise. We didn't spend time stopping bleeding that was caused inadvertently through carelessness, or fixing holes in loops of bowels that were handled roughly or mindlessly. Dr. Brief taught me a powerful lesson. There are two basic approaches to life, the stay out of trouble approach and the get out of trouble approach. In my opinion the former is far superior to the latter.

Okay, so how does this pertain to school? Well, it's simple. DON'T GET IN TROUBLE! Don't get behind in your work. Don't let your average in a class drop to a C so that you have to spend the rest of the term trying to recover. We have all had those times where we spent the last half of the marking period getting an A on every test, project, quiz, paper and homework assignment only to end up with a B or even a B-, because we had let ourselves get in trouble and then had to bust our tails to get out of trouble. This is a terrible position to be in. If you do a careful and mindful job in a class right from the beginning, you can focus your personal philosophy on staying out of, rather than getting out of, trouble.

CHAPTER 7

ELEPHANT

One of my favorite questions is "How do you eat an elephant?" The answer is simple… "One bite at a time." This is one of the most important concepts for the student to grasp. If the student desires to learn a foreign language for example, like it or not, it's a big job and it cannot be accomplished over night. A new language is big, actually it's huge, like an elephant. One must be patient and disciplined. But where should one begin? Well, in fact one usually begins with the basics, right? Perhaps a few simple phrases like hello, goodbye, how are you, my name is John, etc. Maybe we start at an even more rudimentary level like learning each individual letter of the alphabet… A, B, C, D, etc. Wow, that's a daunting task! How on Earth will I ever be able to truly express my feelings and opinions in a completely foreign tongue? It seems an almost impossible task. But the reality is that you can't swallow an elephant whole and you can't swallow French or German or Calculus or Physics or Chemistry whole either. Those are just the facts. The sooner you accept the facts for what they are, the sooner you can begin the long ascent to the top of the academic ladder.

Being a great student requires patience and perseverance. Each day we read a few more pages of a given subject, we attend another lecture, we practice a handful of problems, etc. This is how it is done, one bite at a time. It takes years of hard work and study to become a learned individual. Anyone who tries to sell you a book on tips, tricks, gimmicks and shortcuts to being a great student is either trying to put one over on you or doesn't know what they are talking about. Now don't get me wrong, this doesn't mean that being a great learner is difficult, because it's not. All of us can read; and, if you can do that you can learn anything. You just have to set aside the time every day to do your work, do your reading, and finish your assignments. If you don't quit and you stick with that process every day, year after year, with time you'll be speaking that second language at a business meeting on the other side of the world. It all begins with the first big bite!

CHAPTER 8

LUMBERJACK

Many years ago, when I was still an adolescent, there was a television commercial which was advertising an educational program designed to help children study more effectively. In the commercial they shared a wonderful concept I have never forgotten. We all know that everyone says that in order to be successful one must work hard. Certainly this is a point I reiterate throughout this book. And without question, I believe that this is true. But, there is an important caveat to this that is immensely crucial to understand. The caveat is that just working hard is not the sole key to achievement.

In this TV commercial the presenter of the program said, "Imagine if we took 2 lumberjacks who were identical twins, with identical strength and identical experience in chopping down trees." "Now," he continued, "imagine that you gave each an oak tree to take down. Assume each tree was the same age, the same diameter and the same hardness. Now, imagine that we give one lumberjack a razor sharp axe and the other a sledgehammer to do the job. Who do you think would be more effective in chopping down their tree?"

Wow! That's a powerful image. Anyone can see that the brother given the sledge hammer may work 10 times harder than the one with the sharp axe but never be anywhere near as effective. That is my purpose in writing this book, to give you the freshly sharpened axe and have you put down your dull heavy hammer forever. That is not to say that felling an oak with an axe is easy, because it's not. Even with the right tool in hand it is a lot of work. But let's do everything in our power to make the job as effortless as possible. By studying the techniques and philosophies outlined in this book, I believe that you will be as efficient and effective as possible in getting accomplished what you set out to do academically. So, come on Paul Bunyan! Keep on reading and let's clear an acre together!

CHAPTER 9

WHO

While a resident at Monmouth Medical Center in Long Branch, N.J., I was the pupil of a wonderful teacher named Dr. Michael Goldfarb. At the time Dr. Goldfarb was the surgical residency program director and later went on to become chairman of the department of surgery. Again, like Dr. Constantinopoulos, he wasn't everybody's favorite flavor; but I can assure you he was a highly intelligent man, a first-rate surgeon and an excellent teacher. He was in his own way a bit eccentric, but I liked this about him.

At the outset of every academic year, which in residency training begins in the month of July, Dr. Goldfarb would sit down with the residents to welcome them and let them know what their responsibilities were. One of the requirements of the Accreditation Council for Graduate Medical Education (ACGME) in accrediting residency programs is research. All academic teaching programs must demonstrate a commitment to ongoing surgical research if they wish to maintain their accreditation. In a relatively small program like ours, research was always on a back burner. It was not a priority of those of us who were there to learn how to perform surgery. The residents wanted to operate and take care of patients on the clinical floors; they didn't want to spend time doing research in the records department and writing stuffy white papers in the library. And worst of all, they did not want to figure out how to dust off their old college statistics skills and apply a two-tailed student t-test to determine whether the data had any real relevance. Research was a drag...operating was cool!

Unfortunately it fell on Dr. Goldfarb's shoulders to remind us at the start of every new year that, like it or not, research was required for the program to remain credentialed and for us to graduate with a diploma. We tried making every excuse why we shouldn't have to do research. Some of our favorite excuses were that we were not in a major university hospital and we had no basic research laboratories, we had no animal facilities to conduct surgical research and none of our professors had any grants to fund research. Hearing these objections, Dr. Goldfarb would ask the first year residents in the group the following question, "Who, what, why, when, where or how." It doesn't even appear to be a proper question at first glance. As I told you, he was a little esoteric by nature. Anyway, after a brief pause and a look of collective bewilderment on the faces of the recent medical school graduates, Dr. Goldfarb would exclaim enthusiastically, "It's always the who!"

This meant it wasn't the hospital that was the problem. It wasn't the program that was the problem. The lack of laboratory space was not a problem. In essence, what Dr. Goldfarb was saying was that the real problem was us! We needed to find ways of being creative. We needed to find questions about contemporary surgery that we could answer on the wards and in the operating theaters of our own hospital. The right questions were there. The answers were there as well. All we had to do was make the effort to think about the challenge before us and solve it. We could not expect to be exempt from research because we were not in a major city or at a huge medical center committed to basic scientific research. We had a responsibility to fulfill the requirement set before us by the ACGME, and we did. Every year we wrote numerous papers which were published in respected national and international peer reviewed journals. He was right, the problem was us, and the answer was us.

The reason I bring this up is because by nature, we love to make excuses for our weaknesses or shortcomings. The academic world is no exception to this general tendency of mankind. It is easy to say to yourself, "I'll never get anywhere," "I'm from a small town." Or you might say, "How can I ever become anyone of importance or accomplish anything of significance, I'm in a crummy school district," or "No one in my family has ever gone to college." Well, think of people like my father who lost his parents at a young age, and through a sincere commitment to study and hard work found his way to America. And he is by no means alone. Millions of men and women have come to this country from all around the world in search of opportunity and have found it here. Still millions more have been born to unfortunate circumstances right here in the United States and have through industriousness, self-confidence and self-discipline achieved great heights academically, personally and economically. If you dig down deep into "who" you really are, you will be shocked by what you can accomplish in your life. I can assure you that it is always the "who" that counts the most. It is not your current circumstances, or your lot in life, but the "who" that matters most. And the most important "who" in your life is YOU. Believe in yourself and there is truly nothing you cannot achieve.

CHAPTER 10

YESTERDAY

As I've described, my father was a great one for adages and aphorisms. One of his many favorites was the following: "Yesterday is gone, tomorrow is not here yet, all we have is today." Nothing could be more true. This realization can set you free. We have all made mistakes in our past, and we should all have goals for our future (much more on this later), but in reality all we ever have, and will ever have, is today. So I strongly suggest you make the most of it. We can't go back and change the decisions and actions of yesterday. Nor can we go forward and have any kind of impact on the future right now. At the same time, we must be patient in receiving the gifts our futures will bring as a product of the good work we do today. The Beatles sang, "Yesterday, all my troubles seemed so far away. Now it looks as if they're here to stay. Oh, I believe in yesterday." There's no doubt that it's a catchy tune, but what a load of garbage philosophically speaking. That way of thinking is just rubbish. I strongly suggest that you don't live in yesterday. Dreamers often live in make believe tomorrows, while the high achievers are focused on living in today. Yes, every day brings with it some new problems, challenges and troubles, but that's okay. Sorry to be the bearer of bad news, but that's just the way it is. Deal with it. But don't panic because winners are problem solvers. They stand up to new challenges and see obstacle as opportunities for personal growth.

Never wish away today, it's all we've got and it happens to be spectacular if you make the most of it. There will always be a new semester. There will always be a new book to start reading although you were just tested on the previous one. There will always be a new subject, another quiz, another paper to right, etc. Never let this get you down. Each of these hurdles will make you stronger in the end. Simply focus on the work at hand and focus on today. Yesterday is gone and tomorrow is not here yet.

CHAPTER 11

BOOK

L et's say it was 1976. That was a cool year to be a kid in America because it was the bicentennial anniversary of our great nation. I was six years old in January of 1976. Six is a great age. There were lots of cartoons, Scooby Doo pajamas, and a Big Wheel in the driveway; what could be better than that? Anyway, I digress. In those years Dad was working hard as a private practitioner in Obstetrics and Gynecology. He was in solo practice, which meant he was on call every night, every weekend, every holiday. That's a tough life, especially when you consider he worked 24 hours around the clock when duty called. To say that Dad was a hard worker would be one of the world's great understatements. He never complained about working though. In fact he took great pride in his work ethic and was never hesitant to share with others that he felt this attitude was virtuous. He encouraged everyone he met to work hard. His children were no exception to this rule.

So let me paint the picture for you. My three sisters and I

would be sitting in the "TV room" watching the tube on a Saturday or Sunday morning around 9:30 or so. When I say sitting, that phrase is being used quite loosely. There was probably a lot of lying around happening. We'd be stretched out on the floor or couch. Sitting was reserved for important jobs like being upright so that one didn't choke to death on one's bowl of fruit loops or Count Chocula. Typically there would be a killer episode of Tom and Jerry or Hong Kong Fui blaring on the TV, when Dad could suddenly be heard walking up the stairway from the garage. Then suddenly as he made the left turn at the top of the stairs, down the hallway toward the kitchen, he'd spot us. It wasn't good. Generally this meant he had been out all night delivering a baby. He hadn't slept a wink or eaten; but we certainly had! As was his custom, he was decked out in a three piece suit, neatly tied laces on his wing-tip shoes, and his tie knot impeccably tightened around his neck. Most men wouldn't have been so well adorned had they been leaving for a wedding reception. But Dad took his role as a physician in the community very seriously and always dressed the part. We, on the other hand, were not always so well appointed. Barefooted and sporting pajama bottoms and wrinkled T-shirts was not my father's idea of high fashion. Typically at this point he would pause briefly in the hallway and barely perceptively shake his head in quiet disapproval. This was followed by a collective, "Hi Dad, how you doin', we were just about to go and do our homework." We clicked off the T.V. and scattered like cockroaches in bright light to get showered, dressed, and on to more productive endeavors. Dad would continue to make his way to the kitchen, where he would prepare and enjoy a glass of Earl Grey tea. Just before we could disappear he would say, "Remember, the book is your best friend."

That was the dagger! Ouch! We were sitting around eating crappy cereal, filled with artificial coloring and flavors with no redeemable nutritional value, like a bunch of little piglets and Dad had been up all night responsible for the lives of a mother and a newborn baby. If that doesn't get you motivated, nothing will.

That was one of my father's favorite mantras, and the unabridged version went like this, "The book is your best friend, it never talks back, and it is always there when you need it." It was a line I have heard more than a thousand times in my life, and what it meant was don't waste time, go and read something. Whenever you find yourself wasting time, or with "nothing to do" or with "no one to hang out with," just remember, "the book is your best friend."

CHAPTER 12

EASY

n my second year of surgical training, I was sent to Memorial
Sloan Kettering Cancer Center in New York City. This was
the big time. This was also a bit imposing as an experience at
first. I mean, let's face it, I was coming from a small surgical residency program in central New Jersey, and this was Manhattan.
As they said in the Wizard of Oz, "You're not in Kansas anymore." Well, it turned out to be one of the greatest experiences
of my life. To my surprise at the time, although it doesn't surprise
me at all now, things in reality weren't all that different than how
they were back at our primary hospital. Again, what was most
important was not how fast one could cut or sew, but rather philosophy. This is a concept I will continue to come back to in this
book, the utter importance of philosophy. How we think, and
what we think, are by far the most important determinants of
how we will live and how successful we will be.

While I was at "Memorial", as it was often called, I had the
great privilege of working under the tutelage of a world-class sur-

geon named Dr. Valerie Rusch. This is an individual I would describe as a dynamo. She was highly intelligent, very well educated, extremely hardworking, exceptional in her technical abilities in the operating room, and totally committed to her profession. She stands out in my mind as one of the most extraordinary people I have ever had the good fortune to know. At the time, I was a second year general surgical resident on her thoracic surgical service. I stood six-feet 2 inches and weighed about 255 pounds. Dr. Rusch was about 5 feet tall and maybe one hundred and twenty-five pounds. Despite our physical size disparity, she was bigger than life in my eyes; and, until one day when she actually spoke directly to me, I wasn't sure she even knew that I existed.

One morning around 6 A.M., this would have been August or September of 1996, Dr. Rusch and I were reviewing some CAT scans in the radiology department when we came across a very difficult case. I somehow got up the nerve to ask her how she dealt with the stress and pressure related to managing such a case. It was the kind of disease process where one could easily lose a patient in the operating room, or in the immediate postoperative period, if things didn't go just right. I can still see her, standing there in the X-Ray department when she turned to me and said, "Always remember, John, nothing hard is ever easy." Eureka! I mean, wow, I can't tell you how much that simple phrase has helped me get through tough times in my life. It's an incredible philosophy. If one accepts this way of thinking, one can achieve almost anything. I suddenly realized that it's supposed to be difficult. Those are just the facts sometimes.

Unfortunately, we are led to believe that with enough education, practice, training, etc., hard things will eventually get easy.

Wrong. Hard things never get easy, that's why they are hard. Now, if you are not well trained, educated and prepared for certain challenges then they are not just hard for you, they are impossible. So that helped me a lot, the knowledge that if I was waiting for hard stuff to get easy, I'd be waiting forever. So here's the lesson for this chapter: School is hard. Reading is hard. Studying is hard. Tests are hard. Calculus is hard. Organic chemistry is hard. So what? The sooner you accept that many of the most valuable experiences in life will be hard, the sooner you'll take on new challenges and grow to be an exceptional individual just like Dr. Rusch. Later this dynamic woman went on to become the Chief of the Department of Thoracic Surgery at Sloan Kettering Cancer Center. And despite her rise to the pinnacle of her profession, I'm sure it hasn't gotten any easier to take on the greatest challenges medicine has to offer and to stay at the top.

CHAPTER 13

SCHOOL

Another one of Dr. Rusch's favorite expressions was, "Every day is a school day and everyone is a teacher." I think this is one of the most instructive sayings there is for any student. What it means really goes back to our fortune cookie concept; if one is ready and willing to learn, they can learn from anyone. My father used to advise me when I was in my residency training days to learn from everyone and anyone I could in the hospital. There is a bad habit that surgeons, and all people of high rank, tend to have. This is the habit of feeling superior to those around them. By taking this arrogant attitude in life, you will not only garner a reputation for being an ass, but you will also miss out on building many wonderful relationships and learning a lot of terrific lessons.

On Dr. Rusch's and my father's advice, I honed the ability to learn from just about anyone. For example, of course I learned a lot about how a mechanical ventilator works in the intensive care unit from the pulmonary and critical care doctors. But, unlike many of my classmates, I also sought education and instruction from the respiratory technicians who would physically care for and make adjustments to the machines. I believe that the combination of theoretical and didactic knowledge I acquired, coupled with the practical know-how I picked up from the "techs" gave me a different level of understanding than my fellow trainees. This in turn ultimately allowed me to do a better job of taking care of patients. If for example, one were to study automobiles, one would want to talk with the engineer, the mechanic, the auto-body man and the gas station attendant to gain a true appreciation for what a car is and how it really works. Try to learn every day from everyone, because every day is a school day and everyone is a teacher.

CHAPTER 14

WORRY

The great American novelist Mark Twain has had many amusing and inspirational quotes attributed to him. One of my favorites, which it turns out was probably never written by Twain is, "I've had a lot of worries in my life, most of which never happened." Whether or not Samuel Langhorne Clemens ever actually said this is immaterial. It remains a great quip with an enormous amount of educational potential. What are worries really? Worries are fears. Fears are ubiquitous in this life, and can be one of the most crippling ailments to society.

The point that Twain was making is that many of our troubles are theoretical and self-imposed on the psyche. These are actually worries and not real problems at all. Please never allow fear to deter you from your potential greatness. A certain degree of apprehension is normal when one considers undertaking a life which has a degree of magnitude beyond the mundane. It is normal to ask yourself, "What if I become a cardiovascular surgeon and the patient doesn't make it through surgery," "What if

I become a pilot and an engine fails mid-flight," "What if I become the Captain of a great cruise-liner and the vessel begins to take on water?" There are innumerable "what if" scenarios that the human mind tends to consider as part of its biological function. These are normal thoughts and concerns, but the great achievers are never deterred by these passing notions. The great achievers say, "I am going to get the best education I can and do magnificent operations to save the lives of people with severe cardiovascular disease." Or, in the case of an incredible individual like Sir Richard Branson, who left school at age 16, "Despite my lack of an advanced formal education, I am going to start Virgin Galactic so that one day, John Q. Public will be able to travel in space!"

Don't let your dreams be smothered by the fear of things which are almost certain to never occur. Deal with the here and now in life, never get caught up in the "what if" way of thinking. As problems arise you will be pleasantly surprised that through years of study and preparation you will put out each fire as a smoldering coal before it can become a towering inferno.

Let's inspect the magnificent words of perhaps the greatest illusionist and escape artist of all time, Harry Houdini. Houdini was quoted as saying, "My chief task has been to conquer fear. The public sees only the thrill of the accomplished trick; they have no conception of the tortuous preliminary self-training that was necessary to conquer fear. No one except myself can appreciate how I have to work at this job every single day, never letting up for a moment. I always have on my mind the thought that next year I must do something greater, something more wonderful."

So, remember that courage is not the lack of fear. Courage is the ability to manage and control fear. Just as you should not expect difficult things to get easy, you should not anticipate that stressful situations will become relaxing. Instead, recognize that through consistent study and preparation you will learn to cope with and handle stressful situations like a professional. In the end, this is really what success is all about. Astronaut Chris Hadfield once said, "Our training pushes us to develop a new set of instincts: instead of reacting to danger with a flight-or-fight adrenaline rush, we're trained to respond unemotionally by immediately prioritizing threats and methodically seeking to diffuse them. We go from wanting to bolt for the exit to wanting to engage and understand what's going wrong, then fix it." When things get tough and you start to question your ability to keep fighting to become a great success, remember the thoughts of these great men and free yourself from the mental shackles that bind you and reach for the stars!

CHAPTER 15

WATER

A nother one of my father's favorite parables was that of the goldfish. The story goes that there is a goldfish swimming frantically in circles and from fish to fish in an aquarium. As he approaches each of the fish in the tank, he says desperately, "Where's the water, I can't see the water, I can't breathe!" as he gasps violently through his flaring gills. The other fish look at him in relaxed bewilderment, with a look in their eyes that says, "What the heck is wrong with this guy? Is he nuts or something?" Finally, the frenzied goldfish comes across one of the fish elders and poses the same question in apparent hysteria, "Where's the water? I can't see the water!" Calmly the old fish says to him, "Relax young one, you are surrounded by water. The water is absolutely everywhere. You are floating in the water." And with that, the little goldfish began to relax. He suddenly realized for the first time that it was true; he was indeed completely immersed in beautiful, clean, filtrated, oxygenated water. From then on, his entire life changed for the better.

Here, the moral is perhaps not so evident at first. Let me explain. The metaphor is simple actually. The aquarium is America, and the water is opportunity. Too many of us make excuses for underachieving. We all have goals that we play out in our own imaginations: who we'd like to be, where we'd like to live, what university we'd like to attend, what profession we'd like to practice, how much money we'd like to earn, etc. In reality, the sky is the limit for those of us who are lucky enough to be citizens of the United States of America. Our forefathers crafted an ingenious system of government, which was actually designed so that we would have every chance in the world to be successful in anything we desired to pursue. This understanding is essential to your personal achievement academically as well.

If you can recognize that you are surrounded by opportunity in this great nation, you will cut through the seas of life like a barracuda, not a goldfish. Take advantage of every resource around you. We all have free public libraries, access to the internet and a plethora of learning tools therein. Essentially all schools provide extra help opportunities with one on one teacher to student environments after school, during study halls or free periods. I only wish I had had Google, YouTube, Khan Academy, etcetera when I was a student. Who would have ever believed that at 2 A.M. the night before a big exam, one could log on to the internet and watch a video of a college professor work out Algebra problems on a blackboard! This was considered science fiction when I was in school. There is really no excuse for any American, at any level of education, to make the excuse that they don't have access to a good education. The material is there. Study it! Take control of your own future and your educational destiny. Don't look for excuses for your poor performance, look for vehicles that will carry you to the top of your class, your profession and your generation. If you can't see it, it's because it's all around you, you're surrounded by it. All you have to do is open up your mouth wide and breathe it in. You, my friend, are surrounded by water!

When my father was in medical school in Shiraz in the early 1950's they didn't have actual chairs for students to sit on in the classroom. Believe it or not, they sat on wooden apple crates for the first 2 years, until the University found funding for proper seating. After 6 years of medical school, he then spent 5 years serving as the medical field officer in a very remote, poor, and underserved part of the country before receiving his diploma. This was mandatory public service required by the government. He would not graduate unless he fulfilled this obligation to the people. During his time performing this duty, he was not given an automobile to travel in to attend to the sick patients. Keep in mind this was a vast geographical region. He was given a donkey as a means of transportation. These are not fictional tales. This was his life. Remarkably, he was happy to have the opportunity to treat the sick and the elderly and live his dream to become a physician. He tells these stories with nostalgia and pride. He doesn't regret those difficult days.

Compare your situation and living conditions to his and ask yourself, "Where's the water?" Something tells me, you'll suddenly see that you are surrounded by it. You are floating in it. Take advantage of it. Swim as far as you can. Drink it in. That's what it is there for.

CHAPTER 16

EXPERTS

In the middle ages, a system called apprenticeship was first developed. A young man or woman was typically employed by a master craftsperson in his or her respective field. This period of education was generally 7 years. Interestingly, this is the same number of years that I worked as a surgical resident. The apprentice was a young person who worked in exchange for formal education in the craft. Food and lodging were also provided. Coincidentally, the word "resident" refers to the fact that historically, the surgical student would "reside" within the hospital where they were being trained. The motivation of the master craftsman in this arrangement was obviously cheap labor. The goal of the apprentice was to one day become a master craftsman and earn a handsome living of his or her own. Between the time the apprenticeship ended and the time one would open their own workshop, one would often work for another master craftsman for a salary. This stage of development was referred to as the journeyman stage. The journeyman would save his money until he had enough of a nest egg to start his own business. Again, modern surgical training tends to mimic this progression in many instances. First the young surgeon trains under established surgeons. Then, he or she takes a job working for another surgeon in the early years of practice. Finally, if successful, they may choose to open their own practice. This is a time honored tradition.

The message here is again straightforward. As a student one must expose oneself to as many experts as one can. For example, in my personal experience I was exposed to perhaps as many as 100 surgeons during my training years. They were all fully trained and almost all Board Certified. They were not all experts though. Experts are experts. You'll know them when you see them. It's self-evident. Of the 100 or more surgeons with whom I trained, you'll notice that only a handful will be mentioned in this book. Now, that's not to say that there were no other experts. There were others, but not many. In fact, no matter what profession or occupation you look at in life, most people are average. That's just the way it is. It's a mathematical fact. If you use 50% as average, half of all the people you will meet in your life are below average. It sounds terrible, but it turns out to be true. If you use academic criteria, like those used for grading in school, we know that a 75% on an exam is a "C". A "C" is average. That's a fair student isn't it? If you know a kid in school who gets all "C"s you'd say he's an average student. Actually, you might even say that about a kid who gets all "B"s. I think that's interesting.

It gets even more interesting if you start to think about certain professions. To say that the guy is an average butcher, baker or candlestick maker doesn't necessarily sound that bad. I mean as long as he or she gets the job done it usually suffices, right? On the other hand, who wants to go to the average heart surgeon or brain surgeon? Who wants to fly across the Atlantic Ocean with the average jet pilot? Who wants their tooth drilled by an average dentist? Not too many of us probably, but in reality I guess that's what we often get. The good news is that average is almost always good enough. Again, that's just a fact. The standards in our country, and in most parts of the world for that matter, are set so high that average is pretty darn good. For that reason, it is exceedingly rare for an airplane to crash into the ocean or for a friend to die during a root canal procedure.

So, what's the point? The point is that one should always strive to be one of the outliers. One should always make every effort to be one of the best. Students should always want to be "A" students. This is a mark of excellence. In order to achieve such lofty status, always seek out and expose yourself to the experts. Experts are everywhere. They are in every field of endeavor. As I said, you will quickly recognize them. Gravitate to them. Befriend them. Do anything you can (ethically that is) to get yourself in their good graces. Let their ways rub off on and influence you. Remember the old saying, "Birds of a feather flock together." Join the flock of experts; leave average, and below average, mentors and companions behind. One of the most fascinating observations I have made in my own experience is that experts love to share. You don't have to ask them for their knowledge. They almost always give it away for free to anyone who will listen. So, if you have a "cruddy" algebra teacher but your friend got the "awesome" algebra teacher, stop by his or her class after school and ask for help. I think you'll be quite amazed at their response to your request for assistance. Usually it goes something like this, "Sure John, I'd be happy to help you with a few problems. Pull up a chair."

CHAPTER 17

BED

We've all probably heard the following classic aphorism, "Early to bed and early to rise makes a man healthy, wealthy, and wise." Well this one is super simple. Get to bed! Believe it or not you need sleep. The physiology of sleep and how it works with regard to complex hormonal and bio-chemical processes within the human body are obviously far beyond the scope of this book. But, suffice to say, those complicated chemical processes are both real and required for optimal mental, psychological and intellectual function. You may pursue your own further education on the details and nuances of that very interesting subject. There is an enormous amount of fascinating reading in the scientific and popular literature on the topic.

Most sources would say that optimally the human mind and body function best with 8 hours of sleep in every 24 hour period. A little more or a little less (an hour or so) probably won't throw too much of a wrench into the works; but, 8 hours is a terrific goal. If you desire academic achievement and scholarly excellence you must rest and refresh your brain. You wouldn't run a marathon with exhausted muscles in your legs. Why would you try to take a French history finally when completed exhausted mentally? It's a ridiculous notion, right? Right! But, we've all done it. Most of us have heard or said the following words: "I'm gonna pull an all-nighter, man." That almost always turns out to be a terrible idea. Now, I know we can all point to a time in our life where it worked, but in general it's a stupid move and only reflects that you were ill prepared going into the exam. Whenever you find yourself in a position that you need to stay up all night in order to study for a test or finish a term paper, this should be a blaring warning signal to you that you have messed up! You should never be in that position again, whether or not you occasionally get away with it. The successful student is diligent in his or her preparation and does not get so far beyond in their studies that such extreme maneuvers need be employed. Keep up with your work day to day, and never fall behind. Set a regular "bed time" for yourself, even if you are an adult. Ideally 10 p.m. is a great time. If you awaken at 6, you will have had 8 hours of healthy sleep and will be rested and ready for a great day. And, yes for those of you who have been paying attention to this book, if you want to make it 5 A.M., I'm okay with that too!

CHAPTER 18

TIME

When I was 19 years old, I began volunteering at Passaic General Hospital in Passaic, New Jersey. This was a hospital where my father had been on staff for many years, and had served as Chairman of the Department of OBGYN. I was a freshman college student at the time, working diligently to get into medical school. I would work in the Emergency Department and in the Operating Room, doing anything that was asked of me. I had no formal medical education at this time, so my duties were basically relegated to transporting patients, and helping out as a "gofer" as much as possible.

At the time, in 1988, the most exciting thing happening at "The General," as it was known to patients and staff, was the relatively new open heart surgery program. This was a really big deal at the time, and the heart surgeons took on almost a rock star status within the institution. Occasionally, when I didn't have much to do, I was allowed to stand in a corner of the open heart room and watch, and listen. It was incredible. I couldn't believe I was there. And in true rock star fashion, the surgeons would often play the Rolling Stones and Led Zeppelin while they worked. Man, I thought to myself, this is f@!*ing cool! I would go home and fantasize about being one of those guys one day. It got to the point where any chance I could I'd find an excuse to be in the open heart room watching surgery. Then I began to tell myself that I would become a cardiac surgeon too.

Around that time, I started to ask more questions about what it took to become a cardiovascular surgeon. Well, what I found out came as an absolute shock initially. Remember, I had just finished 12 years of high school, a year of kindergarten and a year of nursery school. That's 14 years. I had a pretty good run I thought. I was pretty well educated. I had some calculus and physics under my academic belt by that time. I had even taken a course in Russian literature as a senior at Dwight Englewood School. I figured, a few more years, a couple of classes on cutting and sewing and I should be all set for the hot lights and the cold steel of the open heart world. Boy, did I have a big surprise coming! It turned out that I would have to finish up 4 years of college, 4 years of medical school, 5 years of general surgical residency and 2 years of cardiovascular surgical training before I could even go looking for my first job. That meant 14 ½ more years from where I was at the time. That meant I would be 33 years old by the time I finished school. And that was assuming everything went according to plan. That meant no hiccups whatsoever in the timeline. I was also informed that delays, derailments, research years, etcetera, were commonplace in this sort of quest. What the hell? Was this somebody's idea of some sort of sick joke? Suddenly, let's just say, I was less than enthused about achieving rock star status.

After I had this revelation, I sat down one day to discuss my concerns with dear old Dad. Not surprisingly, I found him having a glass of tea at the kitchen table. I sat at the head of the table, which happened to be rectangular. He never sat there. He always sat, and still sits, although he's been retired for about 15 years, one seat to the right next to the wall where the telephone is. He sat there so that he could reach the phone without getting up from the table should the hospital call. Sometimes I think he's still sitting in that seat in hopes that they may call him again for a lady in labor or for a ruptured ectopic pregnancy so he can put on his suit, get in his car, and go off to save the day. Anyway, I said, "Dad, I found out some very distressing news." "Oh yeah, what's that?" he queried. "I heard that it would take me another 14 1/2 years to become a heart surgeon if I did everything perfectly and were to go straight through without any delays." "Yeah, that sounds about right", he said. "So what's the dilemma?" he asked. "What's the dilemma? Are you serious? Isn't it obvious?" I shouted, beginning to become unglued by his apparent calm in what was clearly a crisis situation. "The problem is I'll be 33 years old when I finally become a heart surgeon!" "So", he said, "how old will you be that same year, if you don't become a heart surgeon?"

Wow. That was that. I was stopped dead in my tracks. I had no answer. Check mate. The conversation was over. I got up from the table and walked down the corridor, past the T.V. room where I had consumed so many bowls of Cap'n Crunch in earlier years and to my room to spend some time with my best friend… the book.

The point of this one is self-evident. You can't stop time by deciding you won't live your dreams. Time will pass with or without you fulfilling the goals you have set for yourself. Never let time deter you from achieving your true greatness. Nothing hard is ever easy. Some things take a long time to accomplish, that's okay. Just keep marching forward toward a better version of yourself.

CHAPTER 19

JOE

was probably 13 or 14, an age when adolescent males begin to show up at home with friends who may appear a bit, shall we say, unsavory. Well, one day I showed up at the house with a new buddy in tow. For the sake of anonymity, let's call him Joe. Joe seemed like a perfectly fine fellow to me. Perhaps he was a bit rough around the edges. It's possible he donned more denim and leather than the average 7th grader. It's true it wasn't warm enough to necessitate the red bandana he affixed across his acne-ridden brow. But, I thought at the time it was a nice stylistic accoutrement.

After hanging out in my room for a while and playing in the yard, Joe and I had worked up a bit of an appetite. We decided to head inside for a late afternoon snack. As we walked into the kitchen we were greeted by dear old Dad, who was seated in his customary spot nearest to the telephone. He was softly humming a Persian tune and enjoying a glass of tea with a cube of sugar nestled firmly between his back teeth. A brief exchange between all present parties ensued. A bag of chips was snatched from the pantry; we grabbed a couple of cans of Tab diet cola and said our goodbyes. We then made our way back out to the yard for some 1980's style non-playdate-like rough housing. I didn't think much about the chance meeting in the kitchen until I met up with Dad later that evening after Joe had left.

"Son," my father began. "Yeah Dad?" I replied. "I don't like Joe." What? What was he talking about? Joe was cool. Joe had a red bandana and listened to Meatloaf. Dad didn't know what he was talking about this time, and I was gonna let him know it. "You don't even know Joe!" I retorted. Quietly as always, and without any commotion, my father said, "I knew Joe 40 years ago." As young as I was, I got it. I mean I instantly got it. He meant there has always been a Joe. There will always be a Joe. Now, Joe is a fictional name, but Joe is not a fictional character. He still lives in the same town we grew up in and has had a lot of problems along the way, most of them related to drugs. Keep in mind, Joe wasn't using any drugs at the time, but he didn't pass Dad's "eyeball" test. There was just something about him that spelled trouble in my father's eyes. At that age, I really didn't see it. I just thought Joe was a renegade, but in general a good guy. It turns out we were both right. Joe was by no means a bad guy, but he wasn't a good fit as a friend for me either. Joe and I slowly but surely went our own ways over the next year or so.

The take home message here is, choose your friends wisely. Again, birds of a feather flock together. If you are looking to be an outstanding student and excel academically, look for friends in the places those types of people hang out. Typically that won't be the abandoned shed behind the recreation center in town where Joe and his buddies would assemble while cutting class to smoke cigarettes. This certainly doesn't mean good guys, even brilliant students, can't wear denim and leather. We all know that they can. It also doesn't mean that guys with button down collars, penny loafers and blue blazers can't be drop outs and druggies. They can be. All I'm saying is pick your friends carefully. If you run with a pack of winners, you're a lot more likely to become a success yourself. Recognize the Joe in every crowd, be polite and cordial, and keep moving forward.

CHAPTER 20

WORK

When I became a cardiovascular surgical fellow at the University of Rochester Medical Center and the world-renowned Strong Memorial Hospital, I had the good fortune of meeting an exceptional man. George L. Hicks, Jr., M.D. was the Chairman of the Department and one of my most influential mentors. Dr. Hicks was a tall, handsome man with a shock of salt and pepper hair at the time. He was an intimidating figure to most who knew him. After all, he was running perhaps the most revered department in a major university teaching hospital. I grew to have an extraordinary amount of respect for this man, and he taught me many important lessons inside and outside of the operating theater.

Dr. Hicks, like all of my role models, was an exceptionally hard worker. As Department Chair, he had the authority to come and go as he pleased. As it turns out, he chose to come in early and leave late. He chose to come in on weekends and holidays, when he could have assigned such responsibilities to junior attending staff. When it came to his work ethic, he was an ox.

Every morning he would be in the O.R. by 7:00 A.M., prepared to begin his first of 2 or 3 open heart procedures of the day. Between cases, never a moment was wasted. As soon as he was certain that the patient was stable, he would leave me to close the chest with the rest of the surgical team and he would head to the ICU and floors to make rounds. When this was done, he would return to the doctors' lounge in the O.R., but he was never lounging. He had the staff from medical records bring a wheeled cart filled with charts so that he could complete any outstanding paperwork he had. He was a man on a mission. The moment one task was complete he headed off in a new direction to tackle the next. He had been a college football player so he knew a thing or two about tackling.

One day while I was grabbing some lunch between the first and second case of the day, I sat down next to my mentor as he was rifling through charts and feverishly cosigning notes and orders that the residents had written. "Man," I said, "you really love doing paper work Boss!" He looked at me square in the eye and said, "Lad, I absolutely despise paperwork. That's why I get it done immediately, so I don't have to deal with it anymore."

This was another wow moment in my life. His philosophy was painfully simple and obvious, but so incredibly empowering. It's one of those things where you say to yourself, "Why didn't I think of that." So here's the point for the student looking to become superior in his or her work and results. Have you got a novel assigned in English class? Get it out, read it, and finish it. That's as simple as it is. Can you not stand the thought of those 10 geometry problems you have due tomorrow morning? Well then, start banging them out, one by one, starting right this minute. The sooner you begin the sooner it will be behind you. One thing is for sure, the work is not going to go away on its own or through magic. The longer you procrastinate in getting to it, the more it will pile up and the more disgusted you will be by the magnitude of the task at hand.

The other aspect of this way of looking at things is this: Dr. Hicks is not a super achiever because he likes hard work, he is a super achiever because he does hard work. Let's face the facts; work is a four letter word. The only people who actually like hard work are freaks and weirdos. If you are waiting for a day when you love nothing more than sitting down to a desk full of "to-dos" that are still undone, you better forget it pal. The sooner you realize that winners do what others don't, even though they don't enjoy it, the sooner you'll be able to get the job done as soon as it presents itself, whether you like it or not.

Another lesson I learned from "The Boss" is that there are often things in life that don't seem fair that you are required to do. A perfect example of this was the Advanced Cardiac Life Support (ACLS) certification requirement. When I was a cardiovascular surgery resident under the tutelage of Dr. Hicks, we were required by the University of Rochester Medical Center to be ACLS certified. Now, for those who don't know, this is an advanced form of cardiopulmonary resuscitation or CPR. Now it might make perfect sense to a layperson that a cardiac surgeon should have such certification. But, we residents thought it was ridiculous. We felt that this was needed for paramedics and emergency medical technicians (EMTs) who in comparison had very limited formal education and training. To be frank, we felt it was beneath us.

Keep in mind that we were opening chests every day, putting

people on the heart-lung machine and stopping and restarting the heart. We were performing the most complex open heart operations known to mankind. We were routinely shocking the heart and using sophisticated combinations of potent medications to support heart function. In our minds, asking us to spend a day earning an ACLS card would be like asking an astronaut to get a cab drivers license.

We would have long philosophical debates with Dr. Hicks, explaining our position on the subject. He would listen patiently and say with a wry smile, "I know lads. I couldn't agree with you more. It really doesn't make any sense. But, it remains a fact that it is mandatory, so we're all going to have to go and do what we must." And, in fact, every year he would receive a notice that it was time for ACLS recertification. What he would do should come as no surprise to you at this point. The moment he saw the memo on his desk, he would pick up the telephone and schedule the residents and attendings that were due for recertification to take part in the first available training session. This was always on a Saturday by the way. This was also one of the things we hated about the process. We all had so few days free and if you were fortunate enough to have had that Saturday off, it was now completely shot.

ACLS certification was good for 2 years, so he would have his secretary check who was due for renewal and provide those names to the individual running the course. If he were due, his name was also on the list. He never asked us to do anything he wasn't willing to do himself. This in and of itself is a wonderful demonstration of leadership. He didn't try to use his position of power or authority to skirt his responsibilities.

I found it fascinating that he would sign us up for the first

possible training session. Of course, this makes perfect sense to
me now. I can still remember walking out of the classroom after
we recertified together. I must admit I did have a significant sense
of accomplishment getting my new ACLS card despite it being
so "beneath me". He put his hand on my shoulder and said, "You
see lad, now it's over. We've done what we had to do and now
we don't have to worry about it for another 2 years." I smiled and
said, "Yeah, Boss, I guess you're right."

The point here should be clear. There are things in life we
have to do that don't always make sense to us. That doesn't mean
they actually don't make sense by the way. Sometimes these are
academically oriented responsibilities and sometimes they pertain to other aspects of our lives. Either way, the fact is that requirements are requirements. Trying to justify why the rules are
ridiculous, unfair and inappropriate always takes more of your
time and energy than simply doing what you need to do. I
strongly suggest you follow the example put forth by my wise
mentor. Don't waste any time trying to "fight city hall." On the
contrary, be the first one to fulfill the necessary obligations that
you encounter and be proud of your accomplishments, no matter how big or how small. Come to think of it, I'm quite certain
that John Glenn and Neil Armstrong needed to renew their driver's licenses down at the Division of Motor Vehicles every few
years just like you and me. Now that may not be fair, but it's the
law of the land.

CHAPTER 21

WORM

I would guess that just about everyone is familiar with the old saying, "The early bird gets the worm." What this means is that he
who gets an early start gets the prize. Well I'm here to tell you
that it's more than that. It is certainly true that being early or being
on time is an excellent habit and personality trait. And it is also
true that there may be some rewards associated with being punctual. What is equally important, if not more so, is that there are
more often consequences and penalties associated with being late.

I can give you one real life example I think illustrates this
concept with crystal clarity. If you were to work for me in my
surgical practice, in any capacity, and you are late to work with
any sort of regularity, I will fire you without any hesitation. Employees clock in, and records are kept of this. If a pattern emerges
reflecting tardiness, you will be called into the practice administrator's office and given a warning regarding this behavior and
informed that it is unacceptable and inappropriate. A record of
this meeting will be documented and if the lateness persists, you

will be terminated from your employment with my company. It's that simple. So if you're the type who says, "Well, I don't need to be on time because I'm not looking for any special perks. I'm not looking for a worm. I'm not interested in a raise, a bonus or a promotion so therefore I don't need to be on time," you had better check your thinking, and quickly. That is unless losing your job is okay with you. Otherwise, I don't care where you work, you'd better be punctual.

In my years of surgical residency, this was of paramount importance. Lateness was a standard reason for firing residents or having them repeat a year as another young surgeon would advance in their place. We would frequently awaken at 4:00 A.M. in order to get all of our rounds done and notes and orders written prior to reporting to the operating room. These were mandatory responsibilities and if they were neglected, you would be looking for a new job, period.

Now, in school, we all know the drill. If you're late, a time-honored conversation follows, usually something like this… "Mr. Chuback, why are you late?" "Well Mrs. Jones. I'm sorry but I couldn't find my sneakers and my little brother moved my back pack and," "Excuse me John but I'm not interested in excuses. It is your responsibility to know where your things are" etc. Most of us have been there, right? It's not a fun place to be. This is customarily carried out in front of all of your classmates and associated with a significant dose of humiliation. Of course, if this pattern persists, the conversation is replaced with a trip to the guidance counselor's office, the Principal's office, the detention hall and ultimately suspension or expulsion. That is not a great way to manage an academic career. That's a pitiful way to conduct yourself.

If a student is sitting in the guidance counselor's office being reprimanded, what can he or she learn about geology? The answer is nothing. But your classmates, also known as the competition, will be filling their minds with cute little mnemonics which will help them easily remember the difference between a stalagmite ("g" grows from the ground) and stalactites ("c" comes from the ceiling) so that on test day, they will be sailing through the questions and your academic boat will be sinking nicely. Please, don't put yourself in this very compromised position.

Here's another common scenario. You and most of the other students have arrived on time. The teacher is still awaiting a couple of "stragglers" to arrive. As the teacher awaits those who are late, she may throw those who are present a couple of juicy worms. For example, she may say something like, "While we're waiting for Tardy Tommy to arrive, I thought I might mention that for those of you interested in getting an A on tomorrow's quiz, you may want to look over the Thomas Jefferson quotes as well as important dates in Washington's Presidency. Oh here's Thomas now, why don't we get started." Now that's cool if you're there on time, but it's totally lame if you're Tardy Tommy or Larry Lateness.

So remember, if you are the early bird you get the worm. But if you are the worm and you are late in getting back into the safety of the mud in time, you may get eaten. Build a reputation for being an organized individual who is punctual for every occasion, be it academic, professional or social. Despite what you may otherwise hear, there is no such thing as being fashionably late.

CHAPTER 22

RIDICULOUS

N ow for a subject that is very near and dear to my heart. This chapter is about perceptions, realities, myths and truths. It is an important piece of my personal history and is essential to share with any student with high aspirations.

Let's flash back to 1987. I was a senior at Dwight Englewood School. I was a pretty bright kid. I'm sure I was not going to shatter any I.Q. world records for an individual my age, but I was certainly without any major intellectual handicaps. At that time in my life, my ego was definitely more robust than my ethos regarding hard work. It took me some more years to truly embrace a passion for discipline and scholarliness. I squeezed every inch of distance out of a wink and a smile as I could in those days. But ultimately, as is often the case, this was not enough to fulfill my dreams. I would say that at the time I was on average a B+ kind of guy. I was in many honors and AP classes, but really flew mostly by the seat of my pants, letting whatever intellectual fuel I had in the tank naturally propel me. I wasn't big on pushing myself anywhere near my true limits. My oldest sister, Soraya, had gone to Barnard College eight years earlier, and she had gone to a public high school. I had visited the Columbia University campus up in Harlem on many occasions as her little brother, and was completely enamored with the place. Well, I had decided long before my senior year in high school that I would go to Columbia College. I figured that with good grades and a challenging course load, coming from a very good private Prep school, and possessing an engaging wink and a captivating smile, I was a shoe-in. There was only one minor catch. I was alone in my opinion. I wasn't aware of how alone I was, but let me assure you, I was alone.

I was so isolated in my attitude toward college and my chances of being accepted into a top notch Ivy League school that I didn't even visit any other schools. It seems inconceivable to students going through the process today, but it's a true story. I was completely delusional. Looking back, it's almost humorous. I applied, got an interview, got wait listed and ultimately rejected from Columbia. Wow. This is one of those not so good wow moments. This is a "holy @#$t! what do I do now?" wow moment.

Fortunately, I had sent out another application to a wonderful little Midwestern school called Macalester College. This was on the advice of the Director of College Guidance, Miguel Brito. Incredibly, I had never visited Macalester College. Nor had I ever been to Minnesota. "What difference did it make?" I thought to myself. I was going to Columbia anyway, right? Wrong. I was going to Macalester. Well, once I had licked the wounds of my ego, which at the time resembled a set of badly skinned knees, I was off to the arctic tundra of the Midwest. This was not exactly Manhattan Island. Again, it brings to mind the line, "You're not in Kansas anymore."

Put in simplest terms, this charade turned into a real disaster for me. I got out to St. Paul, sight unseen, and I was totally and utterly unprepared. I had no idea where I was or what I was doing there. For the first time in my life, I was lost. I was homesick and depressed. I did poorly in school, drank a lot of beer with my roommate, and smoked too many cartons of Marlboro cigarettes to count. This was not working out. I was way off course.

I struggled through one semester, calling my parents daily to tell them that I was going to quit college and come home. Mom and Dad encouraged me to tough it out, promising that with a little time, things would get better. They didn't. In retrospect, I should have come home sooner than I did, but ultimately, I did finish the semester and returned to New Jersey for Christmas break vowing never to return to Macalester. I kept my promise. To this day I have not been back to Minnesota.

Now I was in a real pickle. It was Christmas break and Dad said, while sitting at the kitchen table pouring his tea back and forth between the saucer and glass to cool it, "I don't care where you go to college, but you're not taking any time off." Message received, loud and clear. I didn't care either at this point, I was just happy to be home. Now, I had to find a school that would accept me over the Holiday break. I was sure I wouldn't even be able to find an administrator on any college campus. It was time to call my old pal Miguel Brito. Miguel was, and is, a wonderful guy. I was able to go over and meet with him in his office at Dwight Englewood. He hammered out a quick letter and made a few phone calls. I went on three lightning fast interviews. One was at NYU, where my best friend from high school was a sophomore, and my sister Lily had graduated about a year before. So, I was familiar with the school and liked it very much. I mean hey, it was a heck of a lot more like Columbia University than Macalester College. At least it was in the same city! Why I hadn't applied there as my safety school I have no idea. I was 18. I also had an interview at Seton Hall University and Fairleigh Dickinson University. Within 3 days I had been accepted to all three schools. Seton Hall and FDU were happy to take me immediately so I would begin matriculating in the spring of that same year, but NYU said I would have to wait until the next fall.

Well, Dad had made it clear that taking time off was not option so just waiting to start at NYU in the fall was not possible. In retrospect it probably would have been the best move, just so I could have a little time to get my proverbial shit together. Anyhow, I figured I would go to one of the other two schools, both of which were driving distance from my parents' house, for one semester and then transfer to NYU. The ultimate plan was to graduate from NYU. Now the only decision was whether I would go to Seton Hall or Fairleigh Dickinson in the interim. "The Hall" was a good local school. It happened to be about 35 minutes from home. On the other hand, "Fairleigh" was about 5 minutes from home but didn't have nearly as good a reputation academically. In fact, FDU was, like many local "commuter" schools in many communities around the country, the brunt of lots of jokes. It sat along the Hackensack River and was sometimes known as Harvard on the Hackensack, but much more commonly had its name bastardized from Fairleigh Dickinson (the name of its founder) to Fairly Ridiculous.

Wait a minute; I was a recent graduate of the prestigious Dwight Englewood School! Was I really considering attending

Fairly Ridiculous? Could this even be possible? It was. Because of the convenience, combined with my inherent laziness, I chose to go to FDU which was only a few minutes away. What harm could it cause, I thought to myself; it's just one semester. And then… the word got out amongst my friends that I was going to Fairleigh. The response was not favorable. "Are you insane," one close friend who was a fellow "Dwightie" said over the telephone from his dorm room at Dartmouth, "You're planning to go to medical school. You can never get into medical school from there!" I had started a bit of a panic in my circle of friends. I guess in retrospect it's nice that they were truly concerned, but their concerns, it turned out, were unfounded.

What happened after this came as a complete surprise to even me. I started at Fairleigh Dickinson University's Teaneck/Hackensack Campus in the spring of 1998 as a second semester freshman and almost immediately fell in love with the place. I was completely at peace. I lived at home, focused on my studies and became a very strong student. I never did wind up transferring to NYU. I had no distractions, and made a few very close friends who were also interested in doing well academically. We practically lived in the library. My group of friends all wound up going to medical and dental school from FDU. I think in a way we were highly motivated by the fact that no one was going to give us any respect because of the school we went to, so we were consumed with doing exceptionally well, all the time. Interestingly, this was the polar opposite affect that being at a fine school like Dwight had on me. I think there was a part of me when I was there that said, you don't have to get straight A's, everybody knows Dwight is super challenging and that a "B" from Dwight is like an "A" from somewhere inferior. This kind of thinking, despite being ubiquitous, is complete bullshit. In almost every instance, an "A" from "nowheresville" is superior to a "B" from "somewheresville". This is especially true when backed up with great scores on standardized tests like the SAT, GRE, MCAT, LSAT, DAT, etc. This would explain why my oldest sister who was a straight "A" student from Fair Lawn High School was accepted to Columbia University, and I was not despite my prestigious pedigree.

Now, don't get me wrong, although I think Fairleigh Dickinson is a fine school, I am in no way trying to compare it to Harvard or Yale. But, being miserable at Macalester and earning "C"s was not going to get me into the American medical school of my choice. If one can be happy, and get straight "A"s at Stanford or MIT, then that's the holy grail of academic achievement baby. More power to ya! But, for many of us, for me at least, it turns out that there is nothing more important than being at a place you love, working your tail off and getting great grades. I did in fact crush the MCAT. I was in fact admitted to essentially every American Medical School I applied to. Ultimately, I turned down prestigious names like Georgetown to attend New Jersey Medical School in Newark. I lived at home until I graduated. I was the happiest guy in the world. I got married a month later, bought a condominium in Long Branch with my new bride, and never looked back with a single moment of regret.

This chapter has several messages, one of which is don't prepare for college the way I did. I was an arrogant ass and paid the price for it, although things turned out to be peachy in the end. But most importantly, remember that the performance of the student is far more important than the reputation of the school. No one gets a gold medal for failing out of Princeton. Find a place where you can be at peace and perform at your personal best. Be true to yourself in this process. I truly believe that the "fit" between student and school is far and away the most crucial predictor of academic success. If you find the right place for you, the results will be "fairly serious." And I mean that in a very good way.

CHAPTER 23

LAKE

John Bullock was a distinguished, handsome, white haired, blue eyed, physiology professor at the University of Medicine and Dentistry of New Jersey when I was a medical student there. He was a wonderful guy and a gifted teacher. He didn't just teach physiology; he also taught learning. Learning is an important subject which unfortunately most students never have the opportunity to take as a class. Learning wasn't a class at UMDNJ either, but Dr. Bullock taught it if you spent any amount of time around him. He gave pearls and tips on how to take notes, how to review and how to prepare for exams. The concept I'm going to share with you here is one that he shared with us in an extra help session that was designed to get us ready for Step 1 in the United States Medical Licensing Examination (USMLE). This was a monstrous exam, a grueling test of all the basic science you had ever learned. How in the world could one prepare for an examination that encompassed such a massive amount of information? It was daunting to say the least.

A small group of us sat in a conference room one day while Dr. Bullock stood at a white board in the front of the room. He said, "Today we are not going to review physiology for the USMLE, we are going to review how to study for the USMLE." He said, "I'm going to share with you the lake philosophy." What? The lake? Are we going fishing or trying to get a license to practice medicine?

On the board he drew a simple image. It was supposed to represent the cross sectional view of a lake. There was a horizontally situated oval that represented the surface and below that a curved line that represented the bottom of the lake. He said, "The classic mistake that people who fail exams make is that they get too deep. A great test taker prepares by knowing only the surface of the lake." And he was right. I had never thought about it this way before. In fact, I think I had it backwards before.

What does this mean, you might be asking? Well, it turns out that it's once again very simple. When we want to do well on a test we say, "I'm going to study like hell. I'm going to know everything there is to know about everything on this test." Stop right there. If that's your approach, you're making a big mistake. You won't do well using that technique. In fact, you may fail. When a test covers a large amount of material, the most important objective is to get through all of the material. Get across the entire surface of the lake. If all the knowledge known in a given subject is defined by the total volume of the lake forget it. That's way too much for anyone to reasonably ask of a student. All you really need to know is the content of the surface. That, in and of itself, is a lot. If you get caught up trying to get deep into every subject you will exhaust yourself and drown in the material. For example, it is essential that you know that the hemoglobin molecule binds oxygen and that it has four binding sites. But, you do not need to know the angles at which the binding sites sit on the basic structure of the molecule. That information is known to scientists, but is far beyond the scope of what the average physician needs to know about hemoglobin. If you are doing your PhD dissertation specifically on hemoglobin/oxygen binding sites that's a different story, but that's also a different test.

This is a very useful tip for any student who wants to succeed. Don't waste time getting too deep into any one subject on a test. Make sure you skim the surface, knowing the basic facts about everything that will be tested, then and only then, if time permits can you delve deeper into areas where you may have particular interest. But, initially, be certain you've got the basics down cold. I have used this technique to pass all 3 steps of the USMLE, my General Surgical Board Certification Exam, my Thoracic Surgical Board Certification exam, both recertification exams and many others. I have never failed one of these exams. Many extremely intelligent people struggle with them, having to repeat them many times before passing. And, in fact, some people never pass these tests. I have found that this technique works like a charm. These colossal tests tend to be very big, not necessarily very hard. The key is to get through reviewing all the material. It is far better to know a little about everything on the test than everything about some things on the test if you intend to pass. Think like a speed boat, not like a submarine.

CHAPTER 24

WEB

Why does a spider put all that work into building a web? The answer is obvious. It's because it makes it easier to catch flies. I mean a spider could sneak up on a fly resting on a surface and grab him in his many legs and devour him, right? But that's a lot more difficult than sitting comfortably in the middle of the web and waiting for the next meal to strike. Then, all he has to do is crawl over casually, wrap him neatly in silk, put him aside, and save him for a time when he's looking for a bite to eat. I see learning very much the same way.

Many years ago it occurred to me that my knowledge was growing in a manner similar to how the spider web works. Everything I've read, everything I've learned, was like a silky strand of knowledge being laid down to create my personal intellectual web. This starts as only one or two strands very early on. We begin with words like "Mama" and "Papa," and we build from there. The more we learn the more robust and complete the web becomes. And then something magical begins to happen. It becomes easier and easier to lay down new strands because there are so many strands already in place that act as a scaffold to crawl along. The connections between ideas become stronger and our ability to lay out new areas of the web begins to happen faster. And finally, we begin to catch flies. The web becomes so robust and so complex that as we interface with new ideas, new philosophies, new facts, we catch them like flies. Our knowledge begins to expand at an accelerating pace. It's a totally empowering feeling. Novel concepts are captured, processed and integrated with greater and greater facility.

For example, the first time we learn to count from one to ten, it's a real challenge. This is a major concept, assigning a sound or a word to a quantity, and recognizing the ascending value of each word in a specific order. But, in time, we all get it. The next time we do this might be in a foreign language. We go to school and we learn uno, dos, tres rather than one, two, three, but we learn it much faster because we already have the concept. We get it. Now it's simply a matter of assigning new sounds or words to numbers, which is a complex notion which we have already mastered. The alphabet would be the same way. Now consider why the creators of the internet may have chosen the name "The World Wide Web." Interesting, no?

So think of your knowledge base as an ever growing spider web, becoming more and more capable of acquiring and assimilating more and more information. This is a wonderful feeling. The more you learn the easier it becomes. Our ability to learn is seemingly infinite. So keep laying down strands and catching more flies.

CHAPTER 25

TARZAN

As a kid, I really liked Tarzan movies. They were so exciting. He had a nice girlfriend, he was in great shape, he spoke to the animals, and he had that amazing call… "aaaaaahaaaaaahhhaaaaaaaahhhh!" Well, you know what I mean. Anyway, by far the coolest thing about Tarzan was that he could swing through the jungle from vine to vine. What kid didn't want to do that? It looked like so much fun. It turns out that I believe life is like a ride through the jungle on vines hanging from the canopy. How so? Let me explain.

If we look at any highly successful individual, Bill Gates let's say, or Paul McCartney, we say, "Man, I'd like to be him!" There's only one catch. You can't be him, not right now anyway. You see, Bill and Paul started their journeys far away from where they are now, in a completely different part of the jungle. If you read Malcolm Gladwell's fantastic book Outliers (a life changer for me), you will see that Bill Gates started out as a student just like everybody else. He developed a particular interest in computers and computer programming, which were still in their infancy at the time. He became obsessive about programming and spent every opportunity writing code. This "programming vine" led him to the next vine in his life, which swung him to the next and so on. Ultimately, he grabbed hold of the $65 billion vine you might say. You see, you can't just wake up and find $65,000,000,000 awaiting you in the mail box. There is a logical progression that gets you there, one swing at a time.

The same is true for Paul McCartney. In Gladwell's book, he points out how hard the Beatles worked to become the amazing Rock and Roll band that they became. They played endless hours for years in seedy joints in Germany before anyone on this side of the pond even new they existed. They were not overnight successes. It took a decade of swinging through the musical jungle, practicing their sets, perfecting their lyrics, their look and their brand before anyone would take notice. Each step, each performance, each note, was a vine that took them from the streets of Liverpool to Beverly Hills and beyond.

You may like to fly like Superman at light speed over the jungle from one end to the other. Unfortunately we have no choice but to live in the real world. The closest we'll ever get to a super hero is Tarzan. Tarzan didn't have any super powers. Through hard work and determination he developed strong arms, shoulders and chest muscles. You would have to imagine that his hands were heavily callused and his grip was like a vice. That's the way you really get from here to there, through a lot of hard work. So get out your loin cloth and swing, baby, swing!

CHAPTER 26

GREEK

"**I**t's Greek to me." This is an expression that has come to mean, "I don't understand what you're talking about. You might as well be speaking Greek." For example, a patient goes to see his or her doctor, and the doctor reviews the results of some recent blood work. A nice conversation takes place. The doctor explains everything fully, truly to the best of his or her ability, being thorough and taking time to ensure that the patient understands everything. Later that day, the patient gets home and a family member asks, "Did you see the doctor today?" "Yes, I did" replies the patient. "Oh good! Did you discuss your blood test results?" your concerned relative inquires. "We did indeed" the patient answers. "Well, tell me, what did the doctor say about your results" they further ask. "I have no idea," responds the patient, "it was all Greek to me!"

Unfortunately, this is a common sequence of events. The reason for this lack of communication is quite logical though. The patient and the doctor were speaking two totally different languages. That's right, the patient was speaking vernacular English and the doctor was speaking in medical jargon. Yes, he spoke some English as well, but all of the key phrases and terms were in "medicalese." There are lots of these specialized languages out there. There's "legalese," "accountantese," "mechanicese," "electricianese," Chinese, Japanese and many more.

The point is that as a student, at some point I realized that essentially everything we learn as a "subject" or field of expertise is in fact nothing more than a foreign language. Let's take geometry for example. Yes it's a discipline within the broader field of mathematics, but ultimately it's just another language. What is a triangle? A square? A rectangle? You know the answer to all of these. A triangle is a closed shape with three straight sides, right? And there is the old right triangle, isosceles, etc. All definitions for shapes you can visualize in your head. A square is always a rectangle, but a rectangle is not always a square. Did you remember that?

Anyhow, I think it makes things a lot easier when you realize that knowledge is just language for the most part. Yes there are mechanical jobs like mine as a surgeon, where dexterity and manual skills are required as well, but they are dependent on your fluency in the underlying language. In my case the underlying language is medicine. Learning language means new words and their associated meanings. This calls for reading, memorizing and repetition. This is a central underpinning of all learning. If you can learn Spanish, French or German, you can learn architecture, engineering or gastroenterology (literally the science of the stomach and intestines, you see… just a new vocabulary word). Often times we will be amazed to find that the actual concepts in a field like astrophysics are not as mind blowing as we might think, it's simply a matter of associating a proper term with a given idea.

CHAPTER 27

WIND

Jim Rohn was a great business philosopher and motivational speaker. He learned much of his philosophy from his mentor Earl Schoaf. One of the most powerful messages Rohn passed along to his students was Schoaf's concept of managing the wind. Basically the idea is that one's circumstances are like the wind. The wind is something we cannot control directly. In other words, we can't stop the wind, increase the wind, or change the direction of the wind. The wind blows any way it wants. That's just a fact. But what we can do is change the set of our personal sail to make the wind work the best for us. We are all like sail boats on the water, but we don't have to take a haphazard course, dictated by the wind. We must be mariners of our own destinies. We must tack, constantly adjusting to changing winds so that in the end we reach our self-determined ports of call. The seas are not always calm. The wind is not always steady and at our backs. Sometimes we must sail into head winds. Sometimes the wind will be so light we will feel as if we will have to put oars in the water to row our personal boat through life. That's just the way it is. But remember, the wind is what it is. Don't waste your precious time and energy trying to change the wind.

Some people complain about circumstances rather than deal with them. Don't get caught up as a student complaining about teachers, your school, the pop quizzes, or how difficult your statistics class is. I can assure you, no one is going to change probability for you. No one is going to make biochemistry or organic chemistry easier so that you can prosper. These are difficult subjects; they are unfriendly and uncooperative winds. I'm sorry to be the one to deliver the unwanted message, but that's not going to change. To be successful on the vast sea of life, I suggest you set your sail and tack back and forth until you find yourself in the library and at your desk as often as possible. Those are the ports of call which will take you to the most exotic and spectacular places. Accept and embrace the wind for what it is, the force that will drive you forward if you are careful to set a proper sail. Without the wind you will get nowhere and be dead in the water. The wind is all you have. School, tests, quizzes, homework, reading assignments and books are all you have to propel yourself to new heights so you had better embrace them. The sooner you do, the faster you'll get to where you are going.

CHAPTER 28

PARTNERS

My sister Sue practices dentistry and lives in New York City and was also an excellent student. Sue is a very social creature. She loves people and is always surrounded by friends. She's a pack animal, definitely not a loner. Sue is high energy and a leader. She is always the one organizing the next activity, vacation, party or event. Well, she was the same way in school.

Sue and I were both living together at home when I was in medical school and she was in dental school at UMDNJ in Newark. I would sit quietly in my room and study. Often my wife, who was then my girlfriend, would study quietly with me. Diane was working on her Doctorate in Neurochemistry at the time, also at UMDNJ. My preferred environment was quiet and often focused on solitude. On the other hand, to watch Sue study, you would think you were on the set of a game show. She'd have ten friends over to the house. They studied in her bedroom which was downstairs beneath mine. She had all kinds of paraphernalia involved. This included white boards, oak tag paper, scissors, colored markers, music, prizes, ribbons and all kinds of other stuff. She studied the way she lives, as a part of a big group. She loved partners in her preparation. She has always been a very generous person, so she had no problem teaching her classmates and sharing with them what she knew. In so doing she would learn more and also create a noncompetitive environment where they would share with her as well. It was very cool. It was not for me, but very cool. I needed peace and quiet. I preferred solitude. But, hey, you find what works for you.

Now, another one of my father's favorite statements, and as far as I know an original, had to do with partners. My father was in solo practice for the last 90% of the time he worked as a physician. In the very early years he did have a partner. But that did not work out ultimately. If I heard my father say it once, I heard him say it a thousand times: "If partners were good, God would have had one." This was a great line. Now, before anyone becomes offended, let me just say that I am not a religious person and I am quite aware that many people are. I have the utmost respect for everyone and their personal religious choices. So, I am well aware that not all religions believe in one God. Some religions have faith in many Gods. And I am also aware that still other people don't believe in God at all. I'm totally cool with all of that. But for the purpose of this chapter, I think the quote makes a point. Dad was from a monotheistic culture so that quote made sense to him. I think we can all see the point he was trying to make… partnership is hard. Now, some people do very well in partnerships, others don't. Again, we must all find what works for us individually.

How is this important when it comes to school work? Well,

I believe that if you can do what Sue did, more power to you. If you can bring classmates together on a regular schedule, and move through the study material at a pace that works for everyone, and you can organize a group that doesn't have a few "cutthroats" who are there only to take information and never share what they know, then that's amazing. By all means, go for it. In my experience, this is very difficult to do. As always, do what works for you, but there is one bit of caution I would like to share about partners in study groups. Never let your partner impede your progress. In other words, let's say you have arranged for a couple of friends to come over one night to review the conjugation of 20 new French verbs and they don't show up; that doesn't mean you take the night off and wait for the group to reconvene at a later date! If they bail out on you, you still get to work. You must avoid the temptation of becoming dependent on the comfort found working in a group. There is such a comfort. There is a feeling of this isn't so bad because we're all in this together. Well, that's great when it works. But when they shaft you for whatever reason and don't show up, you have to have the discipline and fortitude to get the work done on your own. Often times, this will disrupt the organizational pace of the group and things may fall apart. So that's my two cents on partners when it comes to studying. We are not navigating a cruise ship with a thousand passengers, we are captaining a one man sail boat most of the time. Be prepared for a lot of alone time. Much of your greatest growth intellectually and academically will occur with no one present to witness it.

CHAPTER 29

JOURNAL

Throughout our lives most of us have heard the suggestion that we keep a diary or a journal. And almost all of us ignore that advice. It seems like a lot of work on the one hand, and it seems pretty pointless on the other hand. I felt like that for a long time. I don't feel that way any more. A journal is a very powerful tool. A journal is perhaps the most powerful tool you can add to your personal development arsenal. I can't think of any other instrument that can accelerate one's personal growth faster than regularly writing in a journal.

In reality, what is a journal you may ask? It's very simple. A journal is an empty book. When it comes to a journal your job is also very simple. You are supposed to fill it up. You may be wondering what you should fill your journal with. Frankly, the answer is you can fill it up with whatever you please. There are no rules in keeping a journal. No one will judge your journal or grade your journal. In general no one will read your journal, unless of course you allow it. That's totally up to you. You may have chosen to have a private journal you share with no one. You may have a journal you intend for others, your children and grandchildren for example, to read years later. That's the beauty of it. You can do whatever you like. You can sketch in your journal, write poetry, chronicle important (or not so important) things that are going on in your life at the time, tape in cartoons or articles from the newspaper, etc. You can do whatever you like. The process is therapeutic. It gives you an opportunity to reflect on your life. It's something that most of us need to do more of. It forces you to take stock of where you are, where you seem to be going, and where you would like to be.

Again, this activity is best performed alone. I believe a quiet place is best to clear your mind and put your thoughts and feelings on paper. A journal is a device for organizing yourself. As a student you may use the journal to reflect on how you feel about school, the classes you're taking, your effort, your performance, etc. It will give you a chance to slow down and think more deeply about choices you've made, and changes you may like to make in the direction you are going. Your journals will become an important part of your personal library and in time some of your most valuable possessions. Looking back at, and reading your journals will give you the same feeling you get when you look at old photographs of you, your friends and your family. Many important moments that you would have otherwise forgotten will be captured forever. Keeping a journal is an absolutely wonderful way of life. This habit will add extraordinary richness to your life. Perhaps the most important subject one can ever study is one's self. You may also find it is one of the most complex and difficult subjects you ever endeavor to pursue. But, I can assure you it will be well worth it and pay unimaginable dividends in the long run.

CHAPTER 30

GOALS

Perhaps my all-time favorite definition of any word is the definition of "goals." I don't remember where I learned this particular definition. The definition is as follows: Goals are dreams with deadlines. Dreams with deadlines - I really love that. I mean everyone has dreams, right? Dreams imply something you'd really like to do, have or become one day. But there is also a certain negative feeling that the word dream portends. For me at least, it kind of says this is something I'd really like to do, have or become one day, but it's just a dream so I know it's never going to really come true. That's the major problem with dreams. Dreams are fantasies and tend to occur only in one's mind, not in reality.

Now, goals are something different. But goals aren't nearly as much fun as dreams. Goals are awesome because they are real. Achieving a goal is a wonderful and rewarding experience. But like the word "dream," the word "goal" also carries a negative connotation. The negative aspect of a goal is that a goal requires WORK. As we have already established, work is a four-letter word. In fact most lofty goals require HARD WORK. Uh oh, that's 2 four-letter words in a row. That's never good.

One of the most influential motivational speakers I have ever encountered is Brian Tracy. I have read and studied a lot on the subject of goals. In my opinion, no one does a better job educating students on goal setting and goal achievement. What makes his approach to this vitally important subject so effective is the simplicity with which he approaches it. He says that how you set goals is critical in achieving them. His approach involves the programming of the subconscious mind, through messages provided by the conscious mind to activate the superconscious mind to carry out whatever action is required to bring the goal to fruition. I know, I said it was simple and that sounds like a lot of psychobabble. But trust me, it's simple. Put in layman's terms, you simply have to tell yourself what you want and when and you will automatically and organically come up with and carry out a plan to make it a reality.

His technique for doing this is specific, and it's the best I've ever seen. When working in your journal you would write, in the personal present tense whatever it is that you desire. For example, if you are a high school freshman in 2015, and your goal is to attend Columbia University 4 years later, you would simply write the following in your journal every day: "I am a freshman at Columbia University in September of 2019," or "I receive my letter of acceptance to Columbia University in the Spring of 2019." It sounds incredible but this technique, if practiced faithfully, will work the great majority of the time. As Brian explains in his books, "You become what you think about most of the time." He also answers the most frequently asked question of skeptics which is, "What if it doesn't work?" Mr. Tracy answers this using the Socratic tradition, that is, with another question. He replies, "The correct question is not, what if it doesn't work but rather, what if it does work? What if it does work, and you haven't tried it? Then what will you do?"

Working with a journal and setting goals are the most important tools I know of in terms of changing your personal future for the better. Set deadlines for yourself. Don't be a dreamer. When we call someone a dreamer it is rarely a complimentary remark. Be an individual who sets and accomplishes tasks with regularity. Once one set of objectives is met, get out your journal, ask yourself what more you want from life and when, and then go out and make it happen. When I look back at my old lists of goals, I am truly astonished by how many of them I have actually achieved. In my practice we set goals as a professional group on a regular basis. Roughly every 6 months we will convene and review what we have accomplished and we are all blown away by our ability to accomplish just about anything we set out to do. It's a wonderful feeling and inspires us to set the bar higher and higher as we grow as a team. Please try goal setting. I'm sure it will make you more productive than you have ever been before. What do you have to lose?

CHAPTER 31

SILENCE

We live in a world that is often noisy and hectic. We are generally surrounded by others and caught up in the "rat race." For better or worse, that's just the way it is for most of us. We awaken in the morning and the mad rush is on immediately. There is no time to even think. We shuffle to the shower and begin a robotic routine that is usually non-stop, leaving very little time for introspection or reflection on who we are, where we are, what we want, and where we are going. We bathe, dress, maybe grab some breakfast on the go, try to catch the school bus, the city bus, the train or jump in the car. The commute is a chore and tends to be a chaotic hassle for many of us. We struggle to make it to work or school on time and then break directly into the matters at hand for the day.

This continues straight through a hurried, sometimes unhealthy lunch, the second half of the day and the reverse commute back home. Once back home, there is dinner, some TV, some homework and hitting the sack again. The next morning it all starts again. We often feel like Bill Murray's character in Ground Hog day where every day is a carbon copy of the one before. How can we break this viscous cycle and enjoy day-to-day life a bit more? How can we take control and get a better handle on what we really want out of life and where we want to go? I believe very strongly that the answer is silent solitude.

We all have struggles, problems, obstacles and hurdles in life, and in one way or another we all deal with them. Unfortunately, we often deal with them on the fly and at break neck speed. This is a very inefficient way of doing things. One of the most power-ful tools one can employ is that of silent solitude. What does this mean, you may ask? Well, simply put, the name says it all. Find a place to be completely alone with absolutely no outside audi-tory interference. Find a place to be in total quiet while isolated from others.

The best time to do this, in my opinion, is very early in the morning after a good night's sleep. If you normally rise at 6 a.m. to carry out your typical day, I suggest you rise at five. This is per-haps the best time to work in your journal. Avoid the temptation to listen to any music. This is a time for complete silence. When you create a truly silent environment, you will truly have an op-portunity to think clearly. You need no particular agenda with regard to what you may think about each morning. Just create the time and the environment and thoughts will come, maybe a bit slow at first, but then they will begin to flow like a steady stream of consciousness. You will be amazed with what happens during this period of time. You will have a chance to spend time with the most important person in your life... you. You will iden-tify problems, and come up with solutions to them like never be-fore. In many cases this will be the first time in one's life they have ever had such an introspective experience. It is wonderfully empowering and liberating. As thoughts and ideas percolate to the surface of your conscious mind, write them down. Working from these thoughts, you will begin to organize your life in a new way. Through thinking about who you are and what you want out of life, you will begin to set goals. With time you will watch in amazement as these goals are fulfilled one by one.

So give yourself an extra hour in the morning to sit quietly by yourself and think. Your life is important, you need time to think about it deeply. Which classes do I want to take? What profession would I like to be in? Where would I really like to live? How much would I like to weigh? Am I exercising enough? Do I need a different set of friends? Do I treat my friends and family the way I'd like them to treat me? How much money would I like to make? Where do I want to go to college? Is the "best" college I can get into really the right one for me personally? These are just a few of the infinite questions you may consider and have time to think about seriously. All I can advise is that you try it. If you don't like it, you can sleep in for an extra hour, it's up to you. But that extra hour per day may transform you and your life like no other activity. Be alone and be quiet. Just see what happens.

CHAPTER 32

MOUSE

Some time ago I read the well-known book, Who Moved my Cheese, by Spencer Johnson, M.D. I thought it was an incredible story. For those who are not familiar with it, I strongly suggest you read it. But, in a nutshell what it says is that we are mice living in a maze chasing rewards (cheese). The story is one I relate to well because it reminds me much of my own personal journey. In the book there are a group of mice who find themselves in one corner of the maze where cheese is plentiful, but with time the cheese in that area dwindles and ultimately disappears. This is analogous to what happened to my personal pursuit of wealth in cardiovascular surgery. I traversed a complicated and difficult maze to become a cardiac surgeon and by the time I got there, the cheese was gone. What had once been a highly lucrative field was now considered a relatively low paying field when one considers how difficult the work is and how difficult the maze leading to that area is. I was not alone in feeling disappointed by the amount of cheese that remained in this cor-

ner of the maze; many of my colleagues shared the same senti-
ment. Now don't get me wrong, a cardiac surgeon can still make
a very handsome living, but remember that many of us set out
with rock-star aspirations and ambitions. Everything in life is relative.

In Johnson's book, he goes into how different mice facing
the same situation dealt with the change in their environment.
Some stayed where they were, hoping the cheese would some-
day be replaced by whatever powers controlled the cheese, while
others set a new course (a new sail if you will) to find cheese
along other corridors of the maze. The book is written in the
spirit of a children's story and is therefore a pleasure to read. Despite its apparent simplistic nature, the book carries with it great
lessons. I was one of the mice who left the corner of the maze I
had worked so hard to arrive at, only to set off in a new direction
not really knowing where I was going. For me, like some of the
mice in the story, this was the best decision I ever made.

More recently, I read a book written by Deepak Malhotra, a
professor at Harvard Business School called I Moved your
Cheese. This was a very clever move, writing somewhat of a se-
quel to another author's highly successful work and using a similar and quite provocative title. This again was a wonderful book.
Professor Malhotra picks up on Dr. Johnson's concept of mice
and a maze. He describes two particularly special mice who
question the nature of the maze, how it works, who controls the
cheese, and what its limits are. In the end, one mouse finds a
way to crawl up and over the walls of the maze and actually move
the cheese. And yet another mouse, seemingly the wisest of them
all, in an almost mystical feat walks effortlessly through the wall
of the maze as if it didn't exist at all. The book ends with the

epiphany that the mouse is not in the maze; rather the maze is in the mouse. That's heavy. This is reminiscent of an equally powerful scene from the masterful movie The Matrix in which the child guru informs Keanu Reave's character that the key to bending a spoon with one's mind is the liberating realization that in fact there is no spoon.

The first point I'd like to make here is that you should attempt to read all the thought provoking literature of your time. Of course, you should read the classic stuff as well. Watch intellectually stimulating films by the great film makers of your generation. Go back and watch the classics too. I try my hardest to do this. As you can see, it helps me to construct my personal philosophy. These habits will help you to understand the culture you live in. Don't waste your energy on reading or watching trash; you haven't got time for that. That doesn't mean the material can't be entertaining, it just means it can't be trash. There's a big difference. You'll know it when you see it. Go to your local museum and see as much fine art as you can. Do everything you can to expand your mind and the way you understand the world around you. This behavior is essential in any great student.

The second point here is with regard to Who Moved my Cheese. I encourage you to recognize the maze and master it. Learn the rules of the game and play it well. Figure out who controls your cheese and how you can impact that. Have you ever noticed that the "brown-nosers" and "kiss asses," to your dismay and frustration, tend to do very well? I used to say to myself, "That guy is such a brown-noser, Dr. Jones will never fall for that, it's so obvious he's just sucking up to him. He's just kissing his ass to get ahead." But, invariably, to my amazement it did work. People in positions of authority tend to have huge egos that love stroking. So, if you want to excel in a given class where you may be struggling, show interest in the person teaching it. I'm not suggesting you be disingenuous, but be smart. After all, he or she is the "cheese master." Go for extra help sessions after class, ask for some extra problems to practice, ask if they would read your outline or rough draft to see if you are on the right track. Remember the old adage, "You can catch more flies with honey than you can with vinegar." Recognize the maze, who controls the cheese, and what you can do to get some.

The last point is to forget the maze. I know I just told you to recognize the maze and learn to work within the maze so that it might serve you, but in fact there is more than one maze. There is a maze outside of you and a maze inside of you. The maze inside of you is potentially the most limiting and destructive to your future. This is the maze of self-doubt. This is that part of you that says, "I can't do it," "I'm not smart enough," "I'm not strong enough," "I'm afraid." This is the maze you have to destroy. Knock down its walls and burn it to the ground. Break free of the inner maze; rid it from your conscious and unconscious mind. Set yourself free. You are not a mouse. You are a lion. You are in fact the king of the jungle.

CHAPTER 33

SECRET

Some years ago a book called The Secret was published. This book was wildly successful and received a lot of acclaim. I am not here to stand in judgment of anyone's beliefs or work. This book may have been helpful for many, but it was useless to me. I did read it though. And, I read it more than once. I have the same criticism of the book as many others have had. The problem with the technique described in The Secret is that is says nothing about the role of hard work in achieving success. In my personal experience, which I consider to be vast when it comes to academic pursuits, positive thinking alone ain't gonna cut it baby.

If you think that sitting around and repeating positive affirmations or writing goals in a journal or meditating without taking action and doing the work required is going to get you an "A" on your neuroanatomy final, I have a promise for you… you're going to fail miserably. I'm all for positive thinking and being clear in what you want out of life, but it's simply not that easy. Allow me to share with you one of my favorite aphorisms: "Success is easy, just ask any failure." Success ain't easy kid. Remember what my old professor said, "Nothing hard is ever easy." So keep reading everything out there, but be analytical in your reading; ask yourself if what you're reading makes sense. That reminds me of another thing. Dr. Michael Goldfarb used to run the journal club when we were surgical residents. We would review the surgical articles in the world's most renowned scientific journals and Dr. Goldfarb would say, "Always remember, if the results of the study don't make sense then they are probably wrong." In other words, trust your instincts. If something seems to be too good to be true, it essentially always is. There is no substitute for hard work. Those are the cold hard facts. Deal with it. And, please feel free to tell anyone you'd like that I said so, because it's definitely not a secret.

CHAPTER 34

GENIUS

Children love to use the following excuse for failing to achieve academic greatness, "I'm not smart. Sarah does better than everyone else in school because she's a genius!" My sisters and I were no exception to this rule. We would tell Dad about the geniuses at school and attribute many of our own academic short comings to our apparent lack of genetic intellectual capacity. In short, let me just say, Dad was not buying it. This would set him off into his lecturer mode, a mode that came quite naturally to him. This would bring on the classic A. Chuback, M.D., "There is no such thing as a genius lecture." In fact, my father believes that the concept of the genius is a farce. He convinced us that the reason Sarah did better than everyone was because she was like Dr. Sills, she was out-sitting everyone. He taught us to believe that it was our own lack of discipline, drive, ambition and desire that led to our disappointments, not a lack of cognitive capability. When we protested that Sarah didn't study at all, Dad cleared that up pronto with the following statement, "Sarah is a liar" or "Sarah is a cut-throat." He insisted that while I was eating Frankenberry cereal and watching Fred and Barney yuck it up down at the quarry in my footsy pajamas on Sunday morning, Sarah was conjugating verbs in Latin!

In the end, he had us all convinced that it was all about being organized, disciplined and hard working. We were taught that all people were about the same genetically with regard to our intellect and that those who worked harder were rewarded with better grades. And in the very end they were ultimately rewarded with better professions which paid a lot more money. Ultimately, through experience we all bought into this philosophy and have enjoyed the fruits of our labor as well. It did indeed seem true; I could ace any class if I just worked hard enough. There didn't ever seem to be an exception to this rule. This was a true "aha" moment. This realization puts a student very much in control of their destiny. There were no more excuses. If you didn't perform well on a test, quiz or report card, you knew it wasn't because you were lacking brain power; you were simply not putting forth enough effort.

There is another philosophy regarding genius that I have grown to like even more than Dad's, although his approach served me well for most of my life. The other philosophy when first revealed to me came as quite a shock. It hit me like a ton of bricks and I bought it hook, line and sinker. I think it's a much more optimistic way of looking at the subject. There is a school of thought that takes the opposite position to my father's stance. The other philosophy says, "Everyone is a genius!" Isn't that incredible? What a beautiful way of looking at it.

I love this new philosophy. What this way of thinking teaches us is astounding. We are all born geniuses. But being a genius is worthless if you don't put in the work. Let's look at some geniuses and analyze how they achieved acclaim, success and in many cases wealth. I think you would be hard pressed to find anyone who would deny that Albert Einstein was a genius. Agree? Good. Have you ever heard that Einstein was very lazy? No? Good, me neither. Einstein spent his entire life working on his theories. He spent a decorated career at Princeton University struggling to prove his mathematical breakthroughs and concepts. Proof of his incredible genius would never have existed if it weren't for his undying work ethic. You've seen the photos of the white haired old man still toiling away. In fact, he doesn't look like he took time out for a haircut very often. He doesn't exactly strike you as a guy who strove to be retired at 65, right? Right. Einstein was quoted as saying "It's not that I'm so smart, it's just that I stay with problems longer." Genius in and of itself is not enough.

How about the brilliant financial genius Warren Buffett? I'd say he could have taken the early retirement plan and retired at 60 years of age if he really wanted to (wink wink). But no, at the age of 83 he is still the CEO of Berkshire Hathaway with an estimated net worth of $65 billion and rising. His work ethic is unparalleled. He has been quoted as saying he would wake up at 4:30 a.m. to begin working. That devotion to hard work earned him the nicknames "the Wizard of Omaha" and "the Sage of Omaha." The list goes on and on...Steve Jobs, Bill Gates, Richard Branson, etc. One's true genius can only be revealed through hard work applied consistently over long periods of time.

In closing this chapter, I have good news and bad news. The good news is, it turns out you are a genius. The bad news is, you'll never reap any of the rewards of your genius unless you bust your tail! In fact, if you spend your life being lazy, people may actually mistake you for an idiot.

CHAPTER 35

INVENTOR

Well, I'm sure you're riding high now that you know that someone else recognizes what you've known all along... you're a genius. Before you get too carried away with yourself, Albert, let's take it down a notch and look at things from a realistic point of view. Hey, if you heed my advice in this book and work so hard that your genius comes through and you become a multi-billionaire by inventing the first human transporter, that's amazing. But, don't for a second think you have to be an Einstein or a Gates to have a great impact on the world and live a wonderful existence. You don't.

I am reminded of a very stressful day. It was 2001 and I was sitting in a hotel ballroom with an army of young men and women dressed in dark blue suits waiting to take their general surgical oral board certification exam that morning. A gentleman came up to the podium at the head of the room to welcome us and inform us of the rules and nature of the examination. He explained that we would each proceed individually to a total of 3 rooms in the hotel where we would find a team of 2 examiners seated at a desk. One examiner would be a University professor of surgery and typically the other would be a local surgeon from the Chicago area where the test was being administered. We would spend 30 minutes in each room being tested on our knowledge of handling and managing surgical problems. Needless to say, this was a stress provoking experience. I had gone through 4 years of college, 4 years of medical school and 5 years of general surgery in preparing for this day. I mean, give me a break, I had prepared for 13 years and in 1 hour 30 minutes you're going to test my competence? Can you say "Pressure?"

What happened next was awesome. The professor running the testing day, who I believe was also the President of the American Board of Surgery, went on to say the following after laying out the basic format of the exam: "Ladies and gentleman, before you go off to your assigned rooms, let me give you a little advice on how to approach today's examination. You have all come from fine training programs from around our great country. When answering the doctors' questions today, simply do what you would do back at your home hospital. Don't make any effort to be extra smart today. Just do what you would do if you were taking care of a real patient back in your institution. Remember, there are a lot of really great operations that you have learned. I can assure you, there is no need to invent any new ones today." Wow. That was it. "No need to invent any new ones today." I suddenly felt all of the stress and tension leave my body. I thought to myself, "He's right. I know my stuff. I can do this. They're not looking for any earth-shattering breakthroughs in science or surgery today. They just want to be sure that I am well-trained and that I am a safe surgeon." I proceeded to my assigned rooms and handled the test just as I had been advised. And, I passed. All I needed to prove that day was competence; it is rare that anyone will require you to prove you're a genius. This has helped me tremendously throughout my life as I passed many more exams and built a very successful private practice.

As a student, remember to do the basics and they will take you much further than you could ever imagine. Get good rest, eat a good breakfast, be punctual, pay attention, take good notes, do your homework, ask questions, prepare well for exams and the world is your oyster. You can go as far and high as you like if you stick to these simple disciplines. If you happen to come up with a new idea on the order of $E=mc2$ while you're at it, then bravo to you my friend!

CHAPTER 36

STEAL

Many of us have heard the story of the teacher who says of his pupil, "I taught him everything that he knows; but, I have not taught him everything that I know." This is a very important concept. As students we trust our teachers to teach us everything, but in fact they don't. Some of that is intentional, and some is not. As one progresses in the ranks, this becomes increasingly true. For example, every nursery school teacher shares with their charges the entire alphabet. He or she does not leave any of the letters out. If one goes to school, you get the whole thing… all 26 letters, no shortcuts, no abbreviated versions. Conversely, not every graduate student who studied under Professor Einstein at Princeton walked away with their mentor's full knowledge of mathematics, physics and quantum mechanics. This would be impossible even if he had the best of intentions in sharing his knowledge with his protégés.

My old mentor Dr. Goldfarb trained many a surgeon over a 35-year career. Many of these young men and women later went on to open practices in the same community where he taught and worked. He used to joke, tongue in cheek, by saying, "On my tombstone it will read: He trained his competition." Now, this is a humorous line to be sure, but there was an ironic truth to it. This truth begs the question, if he was aware that these young surgeons would one day compete against him in the market place, did he teach them everything that he knew or just everything that they knew? Again, I think that even with the most noble of intentions, it would be impossible to pass on verbally all of one's knowledge to a pupil despite one's best efforts. And it reminds us of Dr. Sills' remark on day one of residency, "This is not a teaching hospital, this is a learning hospital."

When I graduated from medical school and went off to do my surgical training, my father gave me the following advice. He said, "Steal with your eyes." Now, Dad is a very ethical and honest man. He would never suggest that I steal anything that didn't belong to me, but his point was well taken. In the operating room, for example, if a skilled technician is working, he or she does not have the time to describe or explain every nuance of their body position, wrist action or finger motion. The operating surgeon is often concentrating so profoundly that they go quiet, getting lost in their own thoughts. This is a time for the student to be alert and pay attention. This is when those skills learned in the classroom come in handy. This is not a time to lapse in focus. This is a time to watch very carefully a master at work and steal with your eyes. And, I would advise that you can also steal with your ears. Passing remarks, subtle spoken words and so forth are pearls which if noted well and recorded in your journal may serve you for a lifetime. In this book I am sharing many of the experiences I witnessed in my youth and during my most formative years. I became very observant and an excellent listener. You must learn to listen not only to the words, but more importantly the message. I wouldn't be surprised if many of the vignettes I am sharing with you in this book have long been forgotten by the individual to whom the story relates. We often say things casually in passing that have no impact on our own psyche but may be critically important to someone within earshot.

Hearing is one thing, listening is another. Looking is one thing, seeing is another. A great student must be attentive around wisdom. Remain focused, absorb all you can, and never trust your memory. Get to your journal as quickly as possible to write down what you learn so that it can be yours forever. Of course, today we have iPhones and droids where we can make written and verbal notes any time. I still prefer the physical nature of a good quality journal and building a library, but in a pinch collect information in your electronic device and transfer it later when you have time to reflect. Never do anything dishonest academically like plagiarize someone else's work. But, be a "good thief" by stealing with your eyes and ears.

CHAPTER 37

JUDGMENT

A s a cardiac surgical resident at The University of Rochester Medical Center, I had professors whom I adored and respected, but there were others whom I loathed. This is the nature of being a student. You don't always get to choose your teachers, but you have to put up with them even if you don't care for them personally. Those that I despised will be left out of this book. There is a good lesson there though. The lesson is, you can learn not only from your mentors what kind of a person you would like to become but, just as importantly, what kind of person you would never like to become.

I have already mentioned Dr. Hicks. He was one man for whom I had tremendous respect. Another whom I respected and admired immensely was Dr. George Alfieris. George has come to be one of my dearest friends. He is a world-class technical surgeon and even a better human being. Dr. Alfieris is the current Director of the Congenital Heart Surgery Program at the University of Rochester. He held the same position when I first arrived there 14 years ago. George was a wonderful teacher and I truly loved being in the operating room with him.

I remember several of his philosophies. I have found these very helpful in my quest for knowledge and professional excellence. The first thing that Dr. Alfieris would share with his new resident was this, "You don't know what you don't know." That's a wonderful statement because it is true of everyone. No one can know what they don't know. So in fact it reminds us that knowledge and expertise are not a destination but a journey. In truth, when Dr. Alfieris first said to me, "You don't know what you don't know," I could have replied, "Neither do you." But of course I didn't. He was just trying to make the point that when it came to pediatric and neonatal heart surgery, the field was so new to me that I had essentially everything to learn. As one of my other professors liked to quip, "It must be so nice to have so much to learn." And they were correct; there was a lot to learn. There is always a lot to learn.

Remember, this conversation took place when I was 32 years old. I had learned a lot by then. So, if you sometimes get frustrated that school seems endless, that new subjects keep rearing their ugly heads at you, and the moment you finally get a grip on algebra, they reveal to you that there is a thing called algebra 2, take a deep breath and relax. It does get a little exhausting sometimes. But it's okay, just keep going forward. Keep eating that elephant one bite at a time.

Conventionally, the head surgeon, who is typically referred to as the first surgeon, stands on the right side of the operating table. The assistant surgeon, or second surgeon, stands on the left side. Typically, because Dr. Alfieris was performing complex operations on babies, he would be on the right side and the resident would be on the left. As one would progress over the two-year training period, Dr. Alfieris would allow me to spend more time on the first surgeon's side of the table as I proved my technical and intellectual competence. At some point in the case, George would look over and say, "Whattaya think, Johnny Boy? Ya think you're ready to do the next part of the case?" And I'd say, "Sure, George, I'm ready." Then he'd hit me with his classic line, "Now just remember John, it's only a few steps from that side of the table to this side, but it's a very long walk." This was a very interesting concept. What it means is that when one takes responsibility for a situation, the gravity of the situation changes drastically. When you're an assistant in the operating room, there is very little stress. Conversely, when you are responsible for actually cutting and sewing, things get intense quickly. As a student, set your goals high. Be prepared to step up to the plate in life. Be the captain, not the co-pilot. Be the surgeon, not the assistant. Have the courage to be in charge and take full responsibility for your own life and your own future. Take those critical steps that will take you out of someone else's shadow on the assistant's side of the table and into the limelight of the big shot in the room. Through academic excellence, these kinds of goals will become realities for you. Aim high and never quit.

The last anecdote that George would share, which stands out in my mind as a great lesson for any student, is as follows. Each year, as a new resident would join his team, usually for a three month stretch of time, George would ask his new pupil the following question… "Where does good judgment come from?" Invariably the resident would try to put together some sort of reasonable response but it never quite made much sense and Dr. Alfieris would interrupt by answering his own question with, "Good judgment comes from experience." Hmm, you would say to yourself, that's pretty good. I like that. Then, rapid fire, he would follow up with the second question, "And, where does experience come from?" Again, the young trainee would try to piece together a logical response but would once again be cut short as they weren't really getting anywhere. George would once again answer his own question with, "Experience comes from poor judgment." Sweet! That was a good one. It made sense. You had to make some mistakes and screw a few things up to really understand where the limits were and how to perform like a true expert. It reinforced what I had learned from Valerie Rusch about 5 years earlier. Nothing hard is ever easy. Hard things are difficult. Mistakes would be made and we would learn from our mistakes so we could grow. Now of course in a field like pediatric heart surgery, one doesn't make a habit of making lots of mistakes, but with time such surgeons are as proficient as they are because of indiscretions made along the way. These are called lessons learned the hard way.

We all make errors in our judgments and actions in life. The key is to learn from these moments and use these experiences to become a master in judgment. So, if you are 10 minutes late to school on a regular basis, maybe you should get up 30 minutes earlier. If you have always struggled in math, maybe it's time to suck it up and spend one summer in school catching up and getting ahead rather than repeating the same performance in the next academic year. Whatever you see as your own personal weaknesses, set your new goals high and learn from your past so that you can chart a new course for a superior future.

CHAPTER 38

PREPARE

I n surgery there is a commonly used adage, "Well begun is half done." What this refers to mainly is preparation and organization. Nothing could be truer in school as well. If one is well prepared and organized, any job no matter how large or small is much easier to accomplish with a good result. Now in surgery for example this refers to being prepared for the operation and getting the patient prepared for surgery. Classically this would mean that the surgeon knows the patient's story well. In medicine we call that story the patient's history. The operating surgeon should know the patient's history thoroughly. In other words, how did the patient get to this point, what is his illness, what operations has he had in the past, what medications does he take, what allergies does he have? In addition, a good surgeon will have always reviewed any radiological data regarding the patient's illness prior to surgery. For example, are there any X-rays, CAT scans, MRIs, ultrasound studies etcetera to be familiar with prior to starting the operation. In addition, on the day of surgery, does the surgeon have everything he or she will need available in the O.R.? This may include specialized instruments, certain personnel, blood products and so on. When all of this has been checked and double checked, the procedure may proceed. This begins with basics such as positioning the patient properly on the operating table, arranging the O.R. lights for optimal illumination, and prepping and draping the patient with great care to avoid any microbial contamination of the sterile operative field.

When all of the these preparatory steps are carried out perfectly, the surgeon has optimized the patient's chances for a very successful procedure as he or she moves forth with the more critical aspects of the case. Too often avoidable complications may occur because of poor planning and preparation, not because the surgeon does a poor job with the surgery itself. School is very much the same way. Well begun is half done.

Have you ever been a situation where there may be a test or quiz the next day and at 9 or 10 p.m. you realize you have left something essential like your book or a review sheet in your locker back at school? Well, I know it's happened to me. This is never a happy experience. This poor preparation typically results in a poor outcome the next day. Why does this happen? Not because you lack intelligence but because you weren't properly prepared. Being disorganized, not intellectually deficient, caused you to perform poorly. Sadly, we are judged only on our results. And, in the end, a college admissions committee cannot differentiate between disorganized and stupid. Even if they could, I'm not sure which they would prefer in an applicant.

The point is to treat your academic career like a patient whose life is depending on you. Be well rested when you do your homework. No one wants an exhausted surgeon showing up to the operating room to perform their surgery. Check your book bag twice prior to leaving school for the house or before leaving the house for school. Be compulsive in these habits. Always be certain you have what you need. Determining that you need a certain instrument in the middle of a big operation and realizing it is not available is never a good thing! Organize your papers. Develop a system that works well for you. Try to file papers in a plastic bin in your room and get in the habit of never throwing anything out until the end of the school year. You'll be amazed how many of these sheets of paper may be useful around mid-term or final exams.

Keep a well-stocked supply of instruments in your personal armamentarium. That is, have pencils, erasers, blue pens, black pens, sharpeners, tape, scissors, loose leaf paper, white out etcetera on hand all the time. Don't be the dope that shows up to the test without a pen or pencil. It's a sign of being disorganized, unprepared and disinterested. This will not put you in good standing with your teachers. Conduct yourself like a winner. Act like a professional student. Would you want your pilot arriving on board after a sleepless night and without his or her eyeglasses? I don't think so. Be well organized and well prepared for every situation in school and you will be amazed how much easier everything becomes. If you look back, I'm sure you can think of at least one instance where you could have earned a better grade on an assignment or even a report card if you hadn't done something bone-headed with regard to your readiness and preparedness. Surgeons save lives by beginning operations well. Take the same approach to your academic career and you will sail through school with surgical accuracy. Never forget that well begun is half done!

CHAPTER 39

TOUGHNESS

In today's world many children receive extensive training. I
think that in general that's a good thing. It's become common
to hear people moan and groan about how things have
changed since they were a kid. I'm certainly no exception to that
rule. In fact, in my household it's become somewhat of a running
joke between me and my kids. A sentence will often be ended
with, "Yeah we know Dad, that's because we didn't grow up in
Fair Lawn in the '70's." And we all have a good laugh. But it's
true; I am in many ways who I am because of my personal experiences from childhood. Fortunately in my case I carry with me
almost exclusively good memories of those days. Even some of
the scrappier moments like a few bare knuckled exchanges on
the school yard while squaring off against another young buck,
I recall with an odd nostalgia. I have no regrets. How you earned
your stripes was definitely a bit different back then, even in a
comfortable middle class suburban town. Let's face it; I didn't
grow up in a neighborhood as tough as some areas of the Bronx

by any stretch of the imagination. But, on the other hand it wasn't the insular childhood so many kids are experiencing today.

When I was a child there were no play dates. There was very little, if any, adult supervision of any kind after school. Bicycles were not a toy to be ridden in circles in the driveway; they were a real means of childhood transportation. A bicycle could take you to school, to baseball practice, to a friend's house, to the river, to the fort in the woods, to the park, to another town and on occasion even along or across a major highway. Fortunately, there were few serious accidents that I can recall. There were many minor ones. There were skinned knees and lacerated chins for sure. You haven't really lived until you've taken a set of handle bars in the "solar plexus" during a high speed downhill crash. I figure a fair number of significant injuries were avoided because we were quick and agile due to the reduced weight we carried by neglecting to wear a helmet, and in some cases shoes. There were no helmets of course. This went for skateboarding and roller skating as well. We were well versed in how to fall on your backside or in true emergencies an elbow or shoulder. Falling directly on your head was definitely considered spastic and uncool, so we just didn't do it. It would be too embarrassing. The other kids would definitely crack up if they saw you pull that maneuver.

But let's get back to baseball practice for a second. Most of us played organized baseball, farm league, little league and so forth. One was expected to know how to hit, catch and throw when one arrived at tryouts. Now, my father, being from another part of the world, and not being an athlete any way could not teach me any of these skills. He couldn't ride a bicycle or swim either, but that was immaterial. I learned how to do all these things quite proficiently. I learned from other kids in the neighborhood. We didn't have hitting and pitching coaches. There were no bicycling and skateboarding parks and instructors. We learned to play most sports as a little kid in the street. That's correct, in the street, with traffic. When a car would come, we would use what was commonly referred to at the time as common sense and got out of the street. We did not have a common sense coach or take common sense lessons for $85 per hour. Common sense was at the time, well, common. We depended on natural instincts and followed the example set by the older kids. Typically it would go something like this... a car would be see coming down the street, often by the pitcher if he was facing the oncoming car, or by the batter if the car was coming from the other direction. That person would then yell the code word "CAR!" loud enough for everyone in the "field" to hear. We chose the code word "CAR" because it meant there was a car coming. Don't ask me how we figured out such a complex system but we did, and it worked. With regard to the "field", typically second base would be a manhole cover and everything else was architected around that. Depending on how the street was arranged with regard to the intersection and so on, the manhole cover could be the pitcher's mound or home plate as well.

You might ask what this has to do with being a good student or doing well in school. Well, it has a lot to do with independence, for one, learning from your peers for another, but most importantly it has to do with being tough. Yes, toughness was a big part of day to day life. You learned how to find your way in a pecking order that existed in the neighborhood. You learned how to stand your ground when necessary and exercise good judgment in picking your fights. You learned a lot. It was awesome. I'm sure I'm not alone when I say that I wouldn't trade that kind of childhood for the world.

But things are different now. I'm certainly not suggesting we go back to that way of raising children. And I'm certainly not suggesting children ride bicycles on highways, or without a helmet, or play ball in traffic. It wasn't a good idea then, and it's not acceptable now. On the other hand, mental and physical toughness are assets that I do think come in handy in school and in life outside of school. I believe students should look for ways to stay physically fit, either through organized sports or a personal calisthenics regimen. Activities like the martial arts may be the best to learn discipline, respect, toughness and competitiveness. But other activities like dance may be equally as effective. Having responsibilities at home that come with potential rewards and punishments may also be helpful in teaching responsibility and toughness. These are all suggestions, each parent, child and family can make of them what they choose. All I can say is that doing well in school is tough and is a training ground for "the real world." The real world can be tough as well. Being able to stand on one's own two feet is essential for success. The sooner you take action in your life to do this the better off you'll be.

CHAPTER 40

GOLF

I'm not much of a golfer, but one thing I find really interesting about the game is what occurs at the club face at the moment of impact. Well, without getting too involved in the physics (which I couldn't describe even if I wanted to), the interaction between the ball and the driver is fascinating. From everything I understand about this, the angle of impact need only be off by a couple of degrees for your ball to wind up deep in the woods or on the next fairway.

You see, if you strike the ball well, let's say well enough to send it a couple of hundred yards down the course, assuming there is no spin to bring it back into play, you only need to miss-hit the shot by a couple of degrees and you get a lousy result. I mean it really isn't fair. That's why I don't play. Let's be honest, is that fair? You have missed the perfect connection angle by 2 or 3 degrees and the next thing you know you're digging through pine branches to find your shameful shot. That's too much for me to bear. In tennis, if you shank the first serve, you casually reach into your pocket and take a second serve, not a Mulligan, a respectable second serve. Now that's a sport a man can wrap his arms around with affection. That's a game that has built into it true compassion for its participants. Ah, I love tennis; it's so forgiving. It does require a lot of running though. Sometimes I wish I could ride around the court in a cart!

School is a bit more like golf I think. I mean, did you ever notice that if things get a bit off track early in the year, or in the semester, that with time you have found you were way of course? I have definitely experienced this phenomenon. It's not fair. I mean so what if I failed the first quiz? Does that mean I shouldn't get an "A" if I do better the rest of the term? Maybe not. It depends on how many points that quiz, test or paper was worth and what damage that will do to your numerical average. If we begin our academic careers, even at a young age only slightly off course, in the long run we may find ourselves lost in the woods. This is not a good place to be in life or academically. So, first and foremost be careful with every tee shot. Be cautious not to be lax and mess things up at the beginning of a school year or marking period. Keep your trajectory on the straight and narrow. You don't have to do something egregious to foul up an otherwise excellent report card.

Now, there is some good news about golf. There is, like in tennis, an excellent tool called spin. We rarely hit the ball perfectly flat. That's why it's fun to watch the ball's flight path in the air. Sometimes a tee shot will be headed directly for the woods, off by 15 or 20 degrees! But as you watch the ball, it often almost miraculously comes curving back toward the fairway and lands nicely right down the middle. Normally, this is followed by the person who hit it casually bending over picking up the tee and placing it rhythmically in his pocket as if to say, "I meant to do that. I'm cool." So, sometimes we get lucky, but sometimes we don't. We've all seen the shot that looks like it's headed straight down the middle and we watch it fly holding the trophy pose as the ball cuts through the sky. Then, to our horror something inconceivable happens, our beautiful shot begins to veer toward the dark and dangerous woods! Oh no! This can't be happening, but it is. So, as you well know, spin is a big part of the game and the professional players use it masterfully and to their advantage. They hit cut shots and slices and fade shots at will. They go around, over and through obstacles using the technique of controlled spin. They impart their will on the ball, commanding it to do whatever they like. Of course even the pros, hit an errant shot occasionally. Keep in mind no one is perfect.

So, in school sometimes we need to put a little spin on things. If we see we are going off course in terms of our average in geometry, it's time to buckle down in preparing for the next test or quiz by paying attention in class and doing a thorough job with every homework assignment. We can take advantage of those after school and study hall opportunities to go for extra help and put spin on the ball. We do everything in our power to bring a ball that is headed for the hazard back into play. It's all in the wrist. So, think of school as a game. Use golf, or your favorite sport, as an analogy. Remember, you may be down but you're never out. Do everything you can to correct errors early and often. And remember that small errors if not corrected quickly will wind up being big problems.

CHAPTER 41

SPLINTERS

I have a very dear childhood friend whose father was a self-made millionaire. He was born in Brooklyn, New York in 1926, to parents who were Syrian immigrants. He had no formal education beyond high school. He started working in the quilt manufacturing business, working in a sweat shop right out of school. With time, he worked very hard and saved as much money as he could. He had another friend that he grew up with in the same neighborhood who was on a similar path. They were the best of friends and over time developed a healthy rivalry between them to see who could be more successful.

After years of working hard and saving, Eddie Homsany bought his first quilting machine which he had delivered to a small industrial building in Brooklyn. He started his company there with no employees and worked so hard that he often slept on the floor next to the machine. The next morning he would wake up, have a cup of coffee and start up his one man factory again. This went on until he had more than 200 employees and

200 machines. If that's not an American dream story, I don't know what is. He went on to buy a beautiful home with a swimming pool on the hill in Tenafly, N.J. where he raised 2 boys with his wife. He drove exotic sports cars and had a terrific life. By the way, his childhood friend started a successful business of his own and bought a house on the same street. This, like all the stories in this book, is true.

You may ask yourself, how is this possible? What can explain these classic Horatio Alger like "rags to riches" stories? How does one from such humble beginnings, and seemingly limited skills, become exceptionally successful? Well, according to his son, Eddie's answer was quite simple. He used to say, "Chop wood and splinters will fly!" It's that simple. If you work hard enough, for long enough, good things are bound to happen. You just have to keep choppin'! School is no different. You may begin at the bottom of the ladder, but if you keep reading, keep attending class, keep taking notes, keep reviewing the material, keep asking questions and just "keep on keepin' on" slowly but surely you will gain momentum and start to really take off. Once you get some wind beneath your wings you can really soar. Most successful people I have questioned about their personal journey to success have said things to me that didn't necessarily compute at first. For example, if Mr. Homsany were still alive, I have no doubt he would tell me that it was more difficult to go from one machine to two machines than it was to go from 100 machines to 200 machines. That kind of logic doesn't seem to make much sense initially, but as you grow and gain experience in life, that way of seeing the world begins to click.

In school there are gateways. The gateways act as thresholds but if you can get past the threshold things get easier, not harder.

For instance, it is harder to get accepted to Harvard University than it is to graduate. If you can get your foot in the door, staying in school and getting a diploma is the norm not the exception. By the same token most people accepted to medical school finish. And as they old saying goes, even if you graduate dead last in your class, they still call you Doctor. So whatever your personal goals are, don't let anyone dissuade you. Keep pursuing your own happiness and your own success. It takes hard work but it will all be worth it in the end. Remember to keep chopping wood and you'll soon see the splinters will fly!

CHAPTER 42

BLACKSMITH

Perhaps the most elusive goal of all is achieving balance in life. But balance is a bit of a misconception, I think. When you think of balance you may think of something like the scale of justice, a perfectly stable and static device with no movement. There is a tray suspended from delicate chains on either end of the scale. This is balance. Well, I'm here to tell you that unless you're dead, that kind of balance is not attainable, so don't waste your time trying to achieve it. The real world is dynamic, ever in motion and always changing. Real balance is more like a sine wave oscillating around a flat baseline. There is a certain beautiful wobble in life that one can achieve which is rhythmical and almost harmonious with nature but is never stationary. A good example might be the kind of balance one observes when considering gas molecules in a jar. The molecules are forever moving, bouncing off of one another and finding a new position in space. This disorder is what chemists and physicist call entropy. But, oddly this entropic phenomenon results in a bizarre sort of balanced system of its own. Yes, it's true that the molecules don't become balanced and orderly in a straight line across the middle portion of the jar, but they are ultimately generally well-spaced and the jar is entirely filled from top to bottom and side to side. This is the kind of balance or order I believe one can expect from a well conducted life.

Another allegory that my father used to share was that of the blacksmith. He would simply say, "You should live like the blacksmith, one on the nail and one on the horseshoe." Of course what he meant was that when a blacksmith was shoeing a horse, there were two main objectives. The first objective was to get the shoe on the horse. The second objective was to keep the shoe aligned properly with the animal's hoof, balanced if you will. A well shod horse is a valuable asset. With a healthy horse, one can plow a field and harvest a crop and in the end take that crop to market to earn a living. Ultimately, some extra income could be used to plan a picnic alongside a beautiful lake and your horse could carry you and your sweetheart there by carriage. So you can see the practical value of balance. If on the other hand the hoof is poorly shod, then one may find oneself in possession of a lame horse, no crop, no money and no sweetheart. That would be a shame.

So, balance requires that the job gets done, i.e. we shoe the horse, hence one on the nail. Balance also requires the shoe be straight, hence one on the horseshoe. And this is how we go through life, getting things done but constantly straightening things out as they get out of line. Be a blacksmith of your own path, tap once on the nail, and once on the horseshoe to straighten it out a bit, tap again on the nail and so on. If one thinks that he or she can just drive the nails home without realigning the shoe as they go, they are sadly mistaken. That approach is a prescription for an unbalanced life. Balance implies stability. But stability which is static is not realistic. We need to achieve the kind of stability that a jet-liner achieves through continuous forward thrust, not by sitting idle like a bump on a log.

With regard to school, all of these philosophies apply. Balance academically means studying a varied and interesting curriculum. A combination of mathematics, science, history, literature and foreign language is a classic course load. We often feel off balance when we have to study French verbs the same night we have to memorize the periodic table of elements or the Krebs cycle. Embrace this variability in your education. Realize that in the end, this kind of well-rounded exposure mixed with some extra-curricular activities like, sports, music or drama, will make you a very well educated and interesting individual one day. Equally as important, remember that there will be times when you have a 98 average in one class and a 77 average in another. When that happens, it's time to tap a little more on one side of the academic horse shoe than the other; maybe the 98 slips to a 92 for the sake of bringing the 77 up to an 89. That's the idea of scholastic balance. Try it, and you'll soon ride off into the scholastic sunset.

CHAPTER 43

P

A s I mentioned earlier, my adult cardiac surgical mentor at Strong Memorial Hospital was George "Jeff" Hicks, M.D. He was not only a phenomenal heart surgeon but also had a phenomenally big heart. I owe him a lot for all that he taught me. He was generous in every conceivable way and did things for his surgical protégés that I had never seen before. For example, at Christmas time he bought numerous gifts for every member of the team. This kind of thoughtfulness was otherwise unheard of in my surgical training years. When I was there, every resident received a baked ham, an apple pie and a gift certificate for two at one of the best restaurants in town. But Dr. Hicks was also a thoughtful surgeon inside the operating room. He was equally as generous there. He would allow young surgeons, under close direct supervision, to perform complex open heart surgical procedures.

Fundamental to cardiovascular surgery is the use of a potent blood thinner, called heparin, during the critical stages of the

operation. As you can imagine this could set up a scenario con-
ducive to life threatening bleeding. A standard, yet crucial, part
of any heart operation is reversing the effect of the heparin at the
end of the case and stopping any and all bleeding completely.
Dr. Hicks used to say routinely, "Bleeding is the enemy." He
taught all of us to be totally intolerant of any bleeding at the con-
clusion of high quality surgery. We learned this lesson well. Now,
there is a medication called protamine which is given cautiously
at the end of each procedure to reverse the effects of heparin. It
is essentially an antidote. This drug must be administered slowly
and judiciously because it can have the undesirable effect of low-
ering the patient's blood pressure to dangerous levels. One of the
things a rookie heart surgeon gets to take part in is "drying up"
at the end of a major case. This entails looking for and eradicat-
ing any bleeding points. This may entail the use of electrocau-
terization and careful placement of hemostatic sutures. One of
Dr. Hicks' mantras with regard to this aspect of the surgery was,
"Remember the 3 P's lad. Always remember the 3 P's."

In cardiac surgery the "3 P's" are pressure, patience and protamine. We would hold gentle pressure with a cotton sponge
over bleeding points that could not otherwise be dealt with for
various reasons, give the protamine slowly and wait as long as
necessary until there was an absolutely dry operative field. I can
assure you that many people survive open heart surgery because
well trained surgeons employ the philosophy of the "3 P's." It's a
simple concept but it is highly effective. The most difficult part
is the second "P", the "P" for patience. By nature most people
are in a rush. They are in a rush to finish, a rush to move on to
the next thing, a rush to become a big success, a rush to graduate,
a rush to hand in their test, a rush leave class before they have

fully heard what the teacher had said about the homework assignment and so on. Being in a rush, however popular, is rarely a beneficial approach to things. School is no exception to this truth.

With regard to academic achievement I think there are another "3P's" that are critically important to one's success campaign. These are practice, patience, and persistence. Again, the second "P" may in fact be the most difficult to master. Patience is indeed a virtue, but like many virtuous things it is difficult to conquer. One of my father's favorite words when it came to performing at a superior level in school did not start with the letter P but it was very much related to "Practice." My father's favorite word was repetition. Practice and repetition go hand in hand. Dad would implore us to go over things again and again. This was never more evident than in those formative years where we would come to that infamous rite of passage known as the multiplication table. We would go over the "times table" at the kitchen table while Dad enjoyed a glass of tea. Long after you had mastered a given area of the table, Dad would say, "Again. Repeat it again." I would protest, "No Dad, I'm tired, I've got it, 3 times 9 is 27, I know it!" He would persist, "I know you know it, but it's good to repeat it, say it one more time." This would go on as long as he could convince me not to run away from the table. He was very persistent, which brings us to our last "P."

Persistence is key to success. Persistence means never quitting. As the old saying goes, "Quitters never win and winners never quit." One of the keys to becoming something like a heart surgeon is mastering the philosophy of persistence. Let's face it, when the fast track to a profession is 33 years, it's not a path for people who lack persistence. There are no quitters in open heart surgery. This is one of the most important lessons a student of academic success must learn. It is essential that you just keep coming back for more no matter what happens. As the world renowned football coach Vincent Lombardi once said, "It's not important if you get knocked down; what's important is whether you get back up." If one were to fail a class for example, so what? Try harder. Take it again in the summer, or in the next semester. There is no time limit in your education. Every day is a school day and everyone is a teacher. Read a subject over and over until you have it memorized cold. Don't waste your time worrying about the "brilliant" kid in your class who claims to skim over things once and know the material by heart. If he or she truly has such a gift, then I say good for them. I was never that lucky. The likelihood is that you aren't either. Just be patient, practice through repetition and persist in your efforts. If you follow the "3 P's" you can never be denied your goals in the long run.

When we think of practice it may bring to mind musicians and athletes. Think of a violinist repeating scales and finger exercises. The same image is easy to conjure with regard to a pianist or guitarist. Think of a how many golf balls someone like Jack Nicklaus or Arnold Palmer has hit during a lifetime of practice sessions. I certainly wouldn't be surprised to find out that the number would be in the millions. Do you think that even now, a professional musician or athlete would play without practicing first? Have you ever read about the work ethic and practice routines of basketball greats like Magic Johnson, Larry Bird or Michael Jordan? If you haven't, you should. I strongly suggest you study the biographies and autobiographies of highly successful individuals in general by the way. I suggest you read Andre Agassi's amazing life story in Open. Get a sense of how many tennis balls he hit just as a child against the "suped-up" ball machine his father built for him. It's overwhelming to think about it. I refer you again to Malcolm Gladwell's terrific book, Outliers and his description of what he calls the 10,000 hour rule. Gladwell suggests it takes at least 10,000 hours of practice to become a true expert at any given vocation or avocation. I would certainly agree. I know that in the field of surgery I definitely logged my 10,000 hours. I put in 100-120 hours per week for 7 years. Do the math. Okay, I'll do it for you. I had 3 weeks of vacation every year. That left 49 work weeks. Let's be conservative and say that I worked an average of 100 hours per week. 100 h/w X 49w = 4,900 hours per year. Multiply that times 7 years and we get: 4,900 X 7 = 34,300 hours. That was a lot of work. It required patience, practice, persistence, pressure, more patience, and protamine. But hey, as Dad said, those 34,300 hours were going to pass whether I fulfilled my goal or not. What dreams and goals do you have that you may be working at right now? The clock is ticking.

CHAPTER 44

JUMP

I have a new neighbor whom I met when my wife and I moved into a new home. His name is Tom Potenza. This gentleman and I haven't known each other long but by all accounts he appears to be a very successful man. He has an astoundingly beautiful home and a terrific family. His life is rich with all the trappings that a highly successful individual might have, including luxury automobiles, a true mansion, a gorgeous swimming pool, vacation properties, fine Swiss wrist watches, etc. He also happens to be a wonderful person who is very low key and down to earth. I have always been fascinated by such people, particularly when they come from humble means and are self-made with regard to their financial success.

I often try to learn more about men and women like him. I have been surprised to find out in my life that many successful people will share their knowledge and experience quite generously if you simply ask them for guidance. I have learned to be very comfortable with discussing the subject of success with successful people in hopes that I may gather some new tools which I can then apply to my own life. Recently, my friend and I were invited to a gathering at the home of another friend who also happens to live on our street. While there I asked him if it would be okay for me to visit him at his office one day because I would love to see his operation. Fortunately for me he was gracious enough to oblige my request. A week or so later we had an afternoon appointment and I stopped by.

When I arrived, I found his offices were in a beautiful complex in a part of town that was home to many lushly landscaped office buildings. I arrived punctually and was taken on a personal tour of the facility. It was spacious and clean, made up of numerous cubicles with simple desks, telephones and computer terminals. Around the periphery of the space there were a few offices, a kitchen, a conference room and so on. So far, there was not much to learn. It was a nice space but nothing I would not have imagined. We then went and took a seat in his personal office and sat across from one another at his desk. I learned a little about his business which was meaningless to me because I had no prior knowledge of his industry. He is in the information technology space. Then I asked him a simple question. I said, "Why do you think you're more successful than other people in your industry?" Without hesitation he looked me in the eye and said, "I have a riddle for you. If there are 3 frogs sitting on a log and the log is floating in a pond and 1 decides to jump in the water, how many are left on the log?" "Alright, I'll bite," I said, knowing that the most obvious answer would be wrong. "Two frogs will be left sitting on the log" I answered. "No," he countered, "there are still 3 frogs sitting on the log, because deciding to jump in the water and jumping in the water are two very different things." Then he continued, "You see, I've been very successful because I was the frog who jumped in the water while others were deciding to jump in, thinking about jumping in, planning to jump in and so on."

"Wow," I thought to myself, "taking an afternoon off from work and coming out to meet with this man has all been worth it." You see, I understood completely. I got his point immediately. I knew that I could use that philosophy to change my life for the better. With all that I have achieved I knew that I had acquired just one more little pearl of wisdom that would make me even more effective going forward. And that's what education and learning is all about. I wasn't there to learn the I.T. business. That wasn't the point at all. I'm a Doctor not a programmer. But what I learned that day has helped me already to implement programs in my practice that I had previously been waiting to do at just the right time. Winners recognize that there is never a perfect time for change. There is never a perfect time to jump in the water.

As a student, be courageous. Take chances when you can. Raise your hand in class and answer a question even if you're not sure it's correct. What's the worst thing that can happen? You may find out you're wrong but you will be engaged in a dialogue with your teacher or professor. He or she will recognize your interest and your participation. Only good things can come from that. Another good thing you can do is be proactive with your work. Be the kind of student who reads the next chapter even though it hasn't been assigned yet. Do all the even problems in the book despite the fact that you were asked only to do the odd numbered problems. Jump in! Go ahead; leave the rest of the frogs on the log. Be a stand out. Never let fear impede your personal growth and forward progress. This is the behavior of winners. Come on in; the water's fine! Ribbit! Ribbit!

CHAPTER 45

MOUNTAIN

Classically there is a metaphor about success of any kind being associated with getting to the peak, the summit, the pinnacle, or the top of the mountain. In the old days, there was a common after school game called "King of the Hill." This was about gaining the high ground. We think of successful people owning a "house on the hill." We think of scaling Mt. Everest as one of man's great achievements of physical, mental and emotional fortitude. This brings to mind the time honored quote from George Mallory, the English mountaineer, who was asked, "Why do you want to climb Everest?" His fascinating response was "Because it's there." He lost his life in June of 1924 in his third attempt to reach the summit. This, it seems, is the best of human nature, the desire to take on great challenges and achieve things that were before thought impossible.

I recently heard a wonderful statement that pertains to this struggle to climb both real and figurative mountains. If there aren't some rough spots along the side of a mountain, it would be impossible to climb. Isn't that so true? If there aren't some outcroppings and crags on which to step and hold, how could anyone ascend? We need some resistance to push off of and against in trying to make the climb in life. School is no different. There will be some rough spots. That's okay. You may even slip and fall, losing some altitude and forward progress at times. Fortunately, for most of us the mountain metaphor is just that, a metaphor. We won't run out of oxygen as we approach the apex of our academic climb; nor will we swallowed up by a crevasse. Tragically, Mallory died 800 vertical feet from the top of Everest, but fortunately no one dies from homework.

If a mountain were made of nothing but perfectly smooth ice and you were without a pick axe and spiked shoes, you could never make any progress upward. Fortunately, it turns out that life's rough spots actually help us to climb and get where we want to go. It doesn't always feel this way when you're getting hit with multiple homework assignments, term papers to write and tests to take, but it is these hard outcroppings that will actually give you the foothold you need to rise above the rest. Oh, and when you get there, the view is absolutely magnificent. So keep on climbing toward the rarefied air no matter how difficult it gets.

CHAPTER 46

STEPS

M y old friend George Alfieris had a simplistic approach to the complex subject of pediatric cardiac anatomy, physiology and surgery. His attitude to doing world class work and achieving world class results was based on the following philosophy, "If you want to perform a perfect operation, you simply perform every step of the operation perfectly." Sounds easy enough, right? Well yes, but perhaps that's oversimplified, no? No. In fact it turns out to be true. If one begins with the perfect diagnosis and understanding of the problem coupled with a perfect plan, one is off to a perfect start. From there the steps proceed something like this… perfect positioning of the patient on the operating table, followed by perfect placement of intravenous lines, followed by perfect prepping and draping of the patient, the perfect adjustment of the overhead lights, then a perfect incision, then perfect control of bleeding after the incision and so on and so forth. The operation only becomes imperfect when something imperfect occurs and is allowed to persist without correction prior to going on to the next step in the procedure. That's how it is done in surgery; and that's how it should be done in school.

On the first day of school, one should be perfectly on time with a perfectly new notebook and a perfectly sharpened pencil that bears a perfectly intact eraser. On should sit perfectly quietly with one's eyes perfectly trained on the teacher and the blackboard. One should listen perfectly and take perfect notes. After school one should complete one's homework to perfection. If there are questions, these should not be allowed to persist. One should proceed to the internet and search for the answers. If one is still unable to answer these questions, then he or she should seek out extra help the next day and find a perfect solution to their problem. This goes on and on like that forever. If one falls too far behind in school, then problems begin to mount and ultimately the student will have a catastrophe on his or her hands. The same is true for the operating room. If little imperfections in the operation are allowed to accumulate, somewhere along the line these little problems will amount to, or culminate in, big problems. These problems can get so serious that they cannot be reversed or corrected. This is not a good place to be in the operating room, nor is it a good place to be in one's academic career. I think you get my point. Again, no one is perfect. Perfection is not a realistic goal for anyone, but it is a wonderful theoretical goal to pursue. Break things into each of their component steps and big undertakings become much more manageable, just like eating an elephant. The message here is don't just eat the elephant, but wipe the corners of your mouth neatly after each and every perfect bite. Chew carefully, place the napkin nicely in your lap and swallow completely before taking another bite. Practice your manners and you will be able to accomplish anything you put your mind to.

When I was playing high school football, one my coaches pointed out a flaw in a commonly accepted adage. The adage is, "Practice makes perfect." In fact, as he pointed out to us that day on the field, "Practice does not make perfect. Practice makes permanent. If you practice poor technique with poor effort, this will become your habit. These habits, if allowed to persist, can become permanent." Therefore, the philosophy should actually be, "Perfect practice makes perfect permanently."

In school, for example, one can spend hours practicing math problems, but if one is not arriving at the correct solutions, the practice is worthless. We must learn to practice perfection. Again, think of a musician as a good illustration of the point I am making. He or she would never go on stage before an audience until they had practiced the piece perfectly dozens, if not hundreds, of times beforehand. It would be totally unrealistic to think that they could perform the piece perfectly for the first time in front of a crowd. Again, none of us is perfect, but perfection remains a very high standard which we should set as our goal. There is simply no getting around this: the highest quality preparation is required to perform well academically and in every aspect of one's life.

CHAPTER 47

FLIPPER

O kay, I know what you're thinking. You're thinking this is going to be a chapter about a dolphin. That would be cool but I'm sorry to have to disappoint you. Sadly, I have no such story. I do, on the other hand, have an important technique taught to me by the college professor who probably had the greatest impact on me. His name was Professor Vartkis Kinoian. He was a sage. He was possibly the best read man I have ever known. He had gotten his PhD at Columbia University and taught English literature at Fairleigh Dickinson University for many years. I took several of his classes while in college and at that time I was very active in writing poetry. Vart and I would meet on weekends at a diner in Teaneck and go over my latest works. He would critique them and we would have a fabulous time discussing the art of writing over breakfast. We discussed other topics as well. These included fine art, antiques, history, politics and more. It was a great experience for a young man to have a mentor like him. Unfortunately, he passed away some years ago and I still miss his friendship, and mentorship, very much. He would be proud to know I was writing this book, especially since it focuses on education, which is the noble profession to which he dedicated his life and his brilliant mind.

Of all of the actual academic tools Dr. K. shared with me, the concept of page flipping turned out to be by far the most useful. If you are not familiar with the concept of page flipping, it's powerful. Let me begin by saying that this man loved books. He truly loved them. He loved libraries too. He loved the feel of books in his hands. He loved the smell of books. He loved the sounds a book makes when you turn the pages, take them off the shelf from between other books or place them on a coffee table. He loved the quiet of a library, the hushed tones and whispers. He loved traversing the labyrinth of long hallways that make up a university's book stacks. There was nothing about books he didn't love and he was not ashamed to express it. I know all of this about him because he told me so. My father also loves books. Interestingly, I think that in many ways books were Dr. Kinoian's best friends. As Dad said, "They never talk back, and they are always there for you when you need them."

Unfortunately, not everyone has this kind of relationships with books. Many students learn to dislike or even hate books. The idea of a book can bring on a sense of apprehension or even anxiety. Books can be intimidating and imposing. Books can be long and complicated. The contents of books can be challenging and difficult. Some people see books as the enemy. I believe that that is a relationship that needs mending.

In college we took on some heavy stuff as students of Dr. Kinoian. It wasn't the kind of stuff most of us would pack for a day at the beach. This wasn't your typical romance novel or racy thriller kind of material. This was enduring, intellectually demanding, world class literature. In order to encourage young readers to feel more relaxed around these imposing tomes, Professor K. taught us to flip pages. I'll explain now what this truly means. It is exactly what it sounds like; you pick up the book with 2 hands and in a matter of a few minutes flip through every single page. It doesn't sound like much, but trust me it's a wonderfully liberating exercise. It works with any book by the way. It can be technical, fictional, mathematical, scientific or anything under the sun. As I sit writing this chapter in my office, there are numerous heavy, lengthy, hardcover surgical texts that sit just above my eye level on my book shelf. Many of these are 1,000 pages or more in length. Some of these publications are in 2 volume sets. These are books one could spend literally a lifetime studying, and I have. That being said, I could also flip through and glance at every page of Sabiston's Textbook of Surgery in 30 minutes. I just took it off the shelf momentarily to check how many pages it has. I have the 14th Edition and it happens to have 2208 pages. Do you doubt that I could flip through every page in a half hour skimming chapter titles, section headings, images and illustrations? I can. Do you question whether this exercise would have any academic, intellectual, or scholarly value? Well, it definitely would. In fact, it is a wonderful experience.

This one is kind of hard to explain fully. This is an area where you may just have to trust me and try it for yourself. I will try to share with you how this exercise is valuable though. It's like stretching before running, lifting weights or playing a sport. It sort of limbers up your mind and makes the task appear much less daunting. It makes the book feel more like a friend wanting to share with you, rather than an enemy wanting to humiliate and intimidate you. If you've ever blown up a balloon, you'll be familiar with the technique used by seasoned balloon blowers where they physically stretch the balloon several times with their two hands before putting it to their lips. This relaxes some of the elasticity in the rubber so that expanding the balloon with your lungs is much easier. You begin to connect with the book. If it's a subject you know well, like I know surgery; you say to yourself as you quickly flip pages, "Oh yeah I know about gallstones and I know about hernias, this stuff isn't so bad." On the other hand, if it's a book you've never read before on a new subject, you might say, "Hmm... the Pythagorean theorem, I've heard of that, I wonder what that's all about or, Mary Queen of Scots, that name rings a bell, I wonder what was important about her."

Anyway, that's the best I can explain it. If you don't get what I'm saying, all I'm asking you to do is try it once or twice and see if it works for you. If it does, that's terrific; Dr. K. would be thrilled to know I passed the technique along. If it doesn't work for you, hey, no big deal; it's certainly not essential to life. One thing I can say for sure is that when I break out the "flipper" technique when approaching a new book, I have a whale of a good time!

CHAPTER 48

MEMORIES

I once had a teacher who taught me something very profound about memory. Ironically, I can't remember who it was. I'm just kidding. It was Dr. John Bullock, my physiology professor at UMDNJ, the same person who shared with me "the lake" concept of studying. Students, and people in general, often complain that they don't have a good memory. Well, Professor B. had a very different take on this subject. What Dr. Bullock said was that this notion was actually the furthest thing from the truth. He said that in fact it is very easy to remember things and very difficult to forget them. I can still remember some of the specific examples he gave that day.

For starters, he made the case for how powerful the human brain is and what a wonderful computer it is for assimilating, storing and organizing memories. For instance, he said we should consider the behavior of actors in a play. Most actors are not known for their extraordinary academic ability. In fact many actors are quite outspoken about having performed poorly in school and even having dropped out of school. This is in no way meant to suggest that they are not intelligent. In fact they are quite capable intellectually and they prove this ability in their work. Typically they will be given only a few short weeks to memorize an entire play. Often this is work that was previously completely unknown to them. They can memorize not only their part but the parts of everyone on the stage and in the cast. And this is just the verbal component of the memory exercise. They can simultaneously memorize stage direction, body movements, facial expressions and choreography. That is quite amazing when you think about it. These are not super geniuses. These are normal people like you and me. If I were to ask the average person not only to read a book, but to memorize it verbatim they would most likely look at me like I had two heads. It seems like an impossible feat. But, as we learn from the thespian world, it is far from impossible; it is in fact a commonly required aspect of the job. They do it because it is what is necessary and because they have the desire, interest, and drive to do so. So in fact we can see that the typical human brain has an immense capacity to remember data quite readily. There is no arguing that it requires some hard work and effort to read and memorize the material, but the brain's capacity to gather and hold the information is truly quite remarkable.

Now let's look at forgetting. Dr. Bullock made the following argument for how memory works. He said to us, "let's say I gave you the following homework assignment. I'll give you as much time as you need, a week, a month a year it doesn't matter. If you can accomplish one of two challenges, you get a $100,000 reward. The first challenge is to go home and memorize word for word Shakespeare's famous play The Tragedy of King Lear.

When you know it by heart you may come and recite it to the class and receive your bounty. The other challenge is seemingly much simpler. Here, all you need to do is go home and forget your last name. That's it. That's the whole challenge. All you need to do is really concentrate and erase from your memory your family name. It's only one word you need forget. That's not asking a lot, is it? I mean we're talking about a $100,000 prize."

The point here is clear. If there were such an opportunity, essentially all of us could memorize King Lear if we were so inclined. All we would need to do is read it over and over until we had it down pat. But the second challenge is far more difficult. It is in fact probably impossible. I don't know about you, but I found that concept absolutely fascinating the first time I considered it. It had never occurred to me how our minds really work. They are magnificently designed to capture and keep knowledge. They are not designed to lose information. I think that is staggeringly exciting. What a wonderful computer we have all been blessed with. We are all in fact geniuses. Doesn't that make you feel like you can accomplish just about anything you set out to accomplish? It certainly makes me feel that way.

So, the next time you're feeling sorry for yourself because your classmate Albert has a photographic memory and you don't, get over it. You are brilliant and capable of anything. Will you take the time to study and review the material to input the data in your computer? Do you have the drive? Do you have the ambition and the drive? If the answer is yes then the sky is the limit in what you can learn and accomplish in your life. Every student should know that it is much easier to remember than to forget. It just takes a little bit of discipline to take the time to put the data into your own personal super computer.

Before closing this chapter, I have one other idea to share with you. I took one philosophy class in college. It was both interesting and difficult. It was really kind of "far out" as compared to many of the more concrete pre-med courses I was taking so I really enjoyed it. Somehow one day we got on the subject of "photographic memory." This becomes an important idea for many students. We often complain that we have a brilliant friend with a "photographic memory" and that's why they do so well in school and how it's completely unfair, etc. Well, this professor had done a fair amount of research on the concept of photographic memory and felt it was essentially nonsense. He confirmed what we all know. That is, if you really study something well, you may recall quite vividly where in your notes you had read a certain fact or where on the page of the textbook a certain diagram was placed. This is confused for a truly photographic memory. He shared with us a study that was done on individuals who claimed to have photographic memories. The study design was simple. The people were asked what kind of house they lived in. If the participant said a brick home for example, the examiner would then ask, "How many bricks are on it?" The participant would invariably answer, "I have no idea." The examiner would then say, "Well you've seen the house hundreds of times right?" The subject would answer, "That's correct but I have never counted the number of bricks." To this the person conducting the study would say, "Of course you haven't, why would anyone waste their time memorizing something so useless? But, you have seen the house from every side, and you remember what your house looks like. Simply recall the "photograph" of your house in your mind now and count the bricks. I have all day. I can wait for you to count each brick in the "photograph"." Of course, none of the subjects could accomplish this feat, thereby proving that the concept of the photographic memory is a farce. So, next time you're getting down on yourself because you don't think you have a good memory, don't sweat it because in fact you do. It is easier to remember than to forget but no one has a mind like a camera which simply takes snapshots of whatever they lay before their eyes. Memorization takes discipline, time, and hard work, just like anything of any real value in life. A good student learns this and puts in the necessary time to remember the facts needed to excel on a given test or examination. With time the memory of these facts will invariably fade and more relevant facts will come to the forefront of one's consciousness. This is how it goes. Put the work in and your fantastic mind will never let you down.

CHAPTER 49

CALCULATE

Anyone who has ever studied art history has probably seen the famous bronze sculpture by Auguste Rodin entitled "The Thinker." Most everyone has a good image of this classical artwork in their mind. Depicted in the work is a male nude, seated with his chin resting on his right hand. The piece is meant to reflect deep thought and represent the concept of philosophy. I believe in philosophy as it pertains to setting a proper path for one's academic, professional and personal life. The word philosophy comes from the Greek words philos, meaning loving, and sophia, meaning wisdom, hence the love of wisdom. And in the end, isn't that what learning and school are all about? I think so, or at least they should be.

So, I am a strong believer in thinking and philosophy, but there is one other concept that I think is essential to success both academically and professionally. This is the concept of calculation. I have a cousin who lives in Montreal named Khalil Chubin. He has a master's degree in mechanical engineering. Khalil has had a very interesting life and has been extremely successful in business. He has been involved in everything from major road, bridge and infrastructure development in Kuwait, to the importing and exporting of automotive parts, to real estate investment. He seems to have what many people call "the Midas touch" where everything he touches turns to gold. I was recently having a conversation with him about his success and I asked him why he believed he was more successful in business than other people. His answer came as a surprise to me. Without hesitation he replied, "You see, cousin, when other people were thinking about things, I was calculating. Don't be a thinker if you want to be successful; be a calculator." I found that fascinating. Since he is an engineer with a strong background in mathematics, I shouldn't have been surprised he would make such a statement. It made perfect sense that a man with a mathematical mind would conduct his life this way.

Khalil then proceeded to go into some detail with regard to what he meant. All of these examples are not important for the purpose of this book, but they had to do with interest rates, currency exchange rates, tax rates, profit margins and so forth. Much of that is above my head in terms of the specifics, but I got the point. I understood the philosophy of calculation and immediately saw how it applies to academic success. One example Khalil outlined in broad strokes was the following vignette. He said, "You see, you may meet a man who says I think it is a good idea that I get involved in residential real estate. I'd like to be a landlord. I see many other people doing well in real estate. Look at Donald Trump for example. I think that's a good business for me." And, the man may be right, real estate may be an excellent business, but has he calculated the situation or is his thinking too superficially? Here are a few things he should calculate before jumping into a business he knows little or nothing about: how much money does he have, how much of his net worth is he planning to put into such an investment, how much should he spend on a property, how much money will he need to borrow, what are current mortgage interest rates, how many years should he take the loan for, what will be the overall cost of the loan when he is done paying it, how much will he have to pay in property taxes, homeowners taxes and maintenance and repairs, how much does a unit like this one rent for, what will he do if he loses a tenant, how long can he float the expenses without tenants? These are a few of the initial rudimentary calculations one must make before making a decision on whether or not becoming a landlord is wise. For some people the answer will be a resounding yes, for others it will be a disappointing but protective no.

I quickly recognized how I had personally used calculation to be a highly effective student at a certain point in my development. You see, there was a time in my studies that I would think about things, and this thinking would get me into all kinds of hot water. For example, if I had a book to read for English literature class, early on in school I would "think" to myself, "I think I'm going to read that book this weekend." And, sometimes I would and sometimes I wouldn't. It depended on how I felt, what kind of mood I was in, how motivated I was at the time, what other responsibilities I had, what recreational events were available to me, etc. Often, this would lead to big trouble. Procrastination would often get in the way of my best intentions. And then I would find myself with the last 2 days of the 21 days that I had been given to read the book with nothing accomplished. Not only that but it would be the weekend before an essay on the book was supposed to be completed as well. Now, that's a real problem. I found myself in those situations because I had been thinking rather than calculating.

Let me share with you a simple calculation that you can use to your enormous advantage in school. Let's use the example of the book and the essay again. If on February 1st, your teacher, instructor, or professor announces that the class is responsible for reading The Adventures of Tom Sawyer and writing a 1,500 word essay about the book by February 20th; how should one approach this assignment? Actually, the answer is simple. It's an elementary mathematical calculation. Assume your version of the book has 229 pages. Let's also assume we are going to leave the last 3 days leading up to the due date for writing the essay. Typically, this might mean Friday night, Saturday and Sunday. That's fine. What I would do is calculate the problem this way: I have 20 days overall. I will leave 3 days for writing, so 20 - 3 = 17. Therefore, I now know I have 17 days for reading. 229 pages/17 days = 13.47 pages per day, let's call it 13.5 shall we? And, now we know the solution to the first part of the equation. I will need to read 13 ½ pages a day, every day, for 17 days and I'll be finished reading The Adventures of Tom Sawyer. You see how this works? It's not so bad now. Reading 13 ½ pages a day is a snap. Anyone can do that. You don't need to be a genius. But reading 229 pages the final weekend and writing the paper, now that's tough to do even for the brightest student. That would take a genius, and a heck of a lot of time. But we're not done yet. There is a second part to the calculation. We have given ourselves 3 days to write a 1,500 word essay. Now be careful here, this one is easy to miscalculate. The obvious answer seems to be

1,500 words/3 days = 500 words per day. It would seem we could write 500 words per day for the last 3 days and we would be golden. We'd be getting a bit of that "Midas touch" ourselves right? Close, but not exactly. Here's a better calculation. 1,500 words/2 days = 750 words per day. Now I have calculated that I will write 750 words Friday afternoon after school and another 750 words on Saturday. This gives me Sunday to read and review what I wrote, make any modifications and really polish up my work so that it's in perfect form for presenting to my teacher. Now that's solid gold!

Let's look at this example a bit more closely for a moment. There are a few subtleties that I think I should be particular about. For instance, what if something comes up and you were to miss a day of reading. Well, then we recalculate. Recalculating is as important if not more important than performing the initial calculation in the first place. So, what is the recalculation in this case? In fact there a few options. Here's one way of dealing with a missed day: if you are supposed to read 13 ½ pages per day and you miss a day, then the next day you must read 13 ½ pages X 2 = 27 pages. Now, depending on your overall schedule at the time, that may or may not work. This has to be calculated in amongst other obligations. You may be playing a varsity tennis match at another school that day which will eat up a lot of your time. So, please consider another calculation. Let's assume you missed one day of reading on day 10 of your calculated schedule. That leaves 7 days of reading so you can begin writing on pace with your initial timetable. So, a rough calculation is that you need to make up 13 ½ pages in the next 7 days. Let's make it a bit easier and round 13 ½ to 14 pages. You see, you don't need to get out a calculator or a piece of paper and pencil every time you make a calculation. You just have to keep modifying your plan so you remain on track. Fourteen pages amortized over 7 days means an extra 2 pages of reading per day. Now, instead of reading 13 ½ pages per day you must read 15 ½ pages per day so that you can begin working on your essay with 3 days remaining. This is easy. This is not difficult. This is how one manages one's life successfully. One must always be calculating. This obviously does not imply that you don't think or apply your new philosophies toward life; it simply means that you must calculate and recalculate your plan as you go along. If you do this habitually success will come more easily to you in the future. Perhaps if Rodin were still alive, he might create a new bronze sculpture, "The Calculator" a beautifully dressed man sitting at a fine mahogany desk with a pencil in hand ciphering purposefully on a piece of paper. Now, that would be an inspiring work of art.

CHAPTER 50

FOX

I would like to add one last story that was a particular favorite of Dad's. This is the story of the stork and the fox. This is a story of generosity and revenge. One day, a stork came to know a fox that was living in the woods. They seemed to hit it off right away and got along like a house on fire. The stork became so fond of the fox that he invited him over to his home for lunch. The fox graciously accepted the kind invitation and a date was set for their meal together. The stork promised the fox a sumptuous meal of toasted nuts and seeds which happened to be a family recipe for generations in the stork's home. The fox's mouth began to water just thinking of the delicious aroma of freshly roasted warm seeds and nuts. He couldn't wait for the day of their luncheon to arrive.

Well, soon enough the day did indeed come. And being very punctual by nature the fox arrived at the home of the stork right on time. Just as he had imagined, he could smell the sweet aroma of the roasted feast wafting through the door. After a cordial greeting, the stork invited the fox to the dining table. There on the table sat a long narrow necked vase with a bulbous base. The stork smiled at the fox and said, "Dig in!" With that the two friends stood upon the table next to the jar. The stork carefully put his long narrow beak down into the jar and delicately picked up one seed after another and one nut after another. He quickly gobbled them down, enjoying himself nicely. The fox on the other hand was utterly frustrated. He nibbled at the top of the vase with his sharp little teeth and licked around the top of the vessel frantically with his broad tongue, but could not extract a single seed from the jar.

When all the seeds and nuts were gone, the stork told the fox how much he had enjoyed their time together and bid him farewell while showing him to the door. The fox was not pleased but went on his way without expressing his disappointment. In fact, the fox was kind enough to pause briefly at the threshold of the doorway just before exiting and say, "Mr. Stork, thank you for your hospitality, I think it only fair that I invite you to my home for lunch tomorrow. I will prepare for you my mother's famous split pea soup. It is renowned throughout the entire forest." With a full belly and greedy smile the stork accepted the offer immediately.

The following day the stork arrived at the fox's house and could smell the unmistakable scent of split pea soup as he approached on the winding lane that led to the front door. He was greeted by his dear friend the fox. They shared a warm hello and made their way to the dining table. On the table was a large flat platter filled with the most delectable looking soup the stork had ever set eyes on. The fox smiled widely with a glint in his eye and said to the stork, "Please, help yourself." The two stood on the table and with his long broad tongue, the fox began to lap up the soup as quickly as he could. The stork, on the other hand, pecked at the tray of soup fruitlessly, barely even getting his beak wet. Before the stork could protest, the soup was gone. The fox showed the stork to the door and bid him good day. Just before leaving the stork looked at the fox shamefully and said, "Mr. Fox, I have learned a great lesson today. I realize now that I was an inconsiderate and selfish host when I had you at my home for lunch. If you can forgive me, I'd like to have you over again. I really do want to see you enjoy my recipe for seeds and nuts. I will be certain to give you your own portion served in a proper bowl that you can eat from easily." "Of course I'll return to your home for lunch," said the fox, and with that his mother appeared from the kitchen with an extra serving of soup in a tall slender jar for the stork to take home with him. The two remained the best of friends for the rest of their lives.

The message here is perhaps the most important of all. Be generous with your knowledge and your wisdom. Be a teacher as well as a student. The exchange of ideas between classmates, colleagues and friends is the most valuable gift we have to share. The more you give in this area of your life the more you will receive. Share your wisdom if you wish to become wise. I wish you the best of luck in your personal journey toward academic success. I truly believe that the thoughts shared in this book are a wonderful starting place for anyone interested in becoming an excellent student. I encourage you to search for and test techniques that work best for you. This is a very personal quest that each of us is on. It is a lifelong endeavor, which becomes more and more enjoyable the farther down the path we travel. Just keep in mind, there is no true end point or destination. Your capacity for learning and inner growth has no bounds. Embrace your innate drive for success and believe in your own natural ability. This, coupled with hard work, will elevate you to heights you may have previously thought were unattainable. My greatest hope for you is that you can learn to truly enjoy the process of self-development, self-discovery, and intellectual exploration. It's a wonderfully rewarding way of life.